"*Walking in Unity* exemplifies how the power of something small, such as a daily walk, can eventually grow into a flourishing friendship that can overcome tremendous racial barriers. This book is a wonderful example of how two very different people can begin to see each other beyond their caricatures for what

–Robert "Bob" Woodson Sr., founder and president, Woodson Center

"Most books addressing racism come across as clanging cymbals; this one is a symphony of truth and grace. And it provides the only real solution!"

—**Frank Turek,** founder and president, Cross Examined

"There is an amazing amount of clarity in this book—clarity that is desperately needed in the church today. If you read just one book on race and Christianity, make it this one. It will be my go-to recommendation on the subject for a long time to come."

—**Natasha Crain,** speaker, podcaster, and author of several books, including *Faithfully Different*

"Race is one of the most contentious topics in the American church today, and sane discussion and thoughtful biblical proposals are in very short supply. This is why this book is so important and helpful. Calm, practical and, above all, Christ-honoring, this is a volume that Christians should read, ponder, discuss, and apply."

—**Carl R. Trueman,** professor, Grove City College; fellow, Ethics and Public Policy Center

"*Walking in Unity* is raw, authentic, fair, intelligent, and informative, full of solid ideas and personal experiences, and biblical at its core. I have known Monique and Krista for many years (they call me Uncle Jay!), and I have repeatedly been amazed at their wisdom, their knowledge of the issues, their commitment to

Jesus and His Word, and their willingness to tackle the hard issues with a genuine desire to know the truth. Every administrator at Christian colleges and seminaries should be required to read this book. It tackles the main issues dividing us in a readable way. If you had to pick one book to read on race and related topics, this should be it."

—**J.P. Moreland,** distinguished professor of philosophy,
Talbot School of Theology, Biola University; author
of *A Simple Guide to Experience Miracles*

"Monique Duson and Krista Bontrager offer a fresh approach to contentious questions about Christianity and race. This book grows out of their own intense personal conversations, and as a result, their writing is relatable and refreshingly free of trendy buzzwords and sociological jargon. Whether or not you agree with everything they say, you will be drawn in by their common-sense treatment of what the Bible teaches about racial unity."

—**Nancy R. Pearcey,** professor, Houston Christian
University; author of multiple books, including *Love
Thy Body* and *The Toxic War on Masculinity*

"Monique and Krista forged this important, deeply biblical, and well-reasoned book through diligent research and hard discussions about the biblical approach to race in our racially divided times. They address the toughest issues with clarity, charity, and conviction. Bravo!"

—**Douglas Groothuis,** professor of philosophy, Denver Seminary

"Monique and Krista have given us a gracious, biblical, easy-to-read book about what is probably the most volatile and divisive issue in the American church today: race. But this book isn't about guilt, finger-pointing, or anger. It's about unity! The personal testimonies are so real and raw that it left me convicted of my sin, yet full of faith. The cornerstone is that the unity of all believers from every tribe and tongue in the New Man, Christ Jesus—or what the authors call 'the family'—is not something we have yet to accomplish but is already a spiritual reality. The beauty of that truth shines forth gloriously on every page and encourages us to live accordingly."

—**John L. Cooper,** lead singer of Christian rock band Skillet, author of *Awake and Alive to Truth*, host of the *Cooper Stuff* podcast

"This insightful book tackles a difficult subject with wisdom, clarity, grace, and truth. Krista and Monique give us a biblical, not humanistic, understanding of race and racism. *Walking in Unity* is crucial for church leaders and everyday Christians to help us understand and combat the lies that our culture bombards us with daily regarding race. I highly recommend it!"

—**Becket Cook,** author of *A Change of Affection: A Gay Man's Incredible Story of Redemption*, host of *The Becket Cook Show*

"Why aren't Christians, whose God created every 'ethnos' under heaven, leading the national conversation about race? Because they have not yet read *Walking in Unity*. In its pages you will find the biblical, historical, and personal context needed to become the peace-making, reconciling agents for racial unity that God expects His church to be."

—**Katy Faust,** founder and president, Them Before Us

"The Scriptures tell us that all human beings are created in the image of God. Though we may be of different ethnicities, cultures, and physical appearances, we are of one blood. However, in these times of tremendous chaos, confusion, and conflict, as believers, Jesus Christ must be the cornerstone and source of our identity. As we are forgiven of our sins and reconciled to God, then, and only then, can we walk in true unity with each other. Ethnic groups and skin colors don't reconcile. Hearts do! *Walking in Unity* serves as an excellent and timely reminder of these biblical principles."

—**Judge Cheryl Lynn Allen,** first black woman elected to the Pennsylvania Superior Court

"Monique Duson and Krista Bontrager have grappled with the contentious issues of race and unity. They have been breathtakingly transparent in their journey to defining a biblical model of unity, founding each principle on Scripture. Every Christian needs to read this book, take it to heart, and implement the biblical principles laid out herein."

—**Richard G. Howe,** provost, Norman L. Geisler Chair of Christian Apologetics, Southern Evangelical Seminary

"*Walking in Unity* is the guidebook for difficult conversations we need to be having in this moment. Monique and Krista's message and mission are rooted in biblical truth, providing clear, hope-filled, unifying navigation to sensitive and tough issues that is better than anything the world has to offer. They are doing mighty things for God's kingdom!"

—**Cissie Graham Lynch,** Billy Graham Evangelistic Association and Samaritan's Purse

"Monique Duson and Krista Bontrager may be two unlikely friends but are perfectly matched to coauthor *Walking in Unity*. Many 'Christian' approaches to racial reconciliation are essentially secular frameworks with a few Bible verses thrown in. *Walking in Unity* is an invaluable and vital resource. I wholeheartedly commend this book as a guide to address biblical unity and the secular concept of race."

—**Christopher Yuan,** author of *Holy Sexuality and the Gospel*, producer of the Holy Sexuality Project

"Like so many Christians, Monique Duson and Krista Bontrager were drawn together by faith and friendship yet pulled apart by issues of race and justice. Their personal story frames a book that is both powerful and practical. *Walking in Unity* cuts to the heart of discussions of 'antiracism' and 'racial reconciliation' both inside and outside the church. It exposes the unbiblical assumptions that even sincere, well-intentioned Christians can embrace and offers an approach to racial unity rooted in the gospel. I highly recommend it."

—**Neil Shenvi,** author of *Why Believe?: A Reasoned Approach to Christianity* and coauthor of *Critical Dilemma: The Rise of Critical Theories and Social Justice Ideology*

"Fellow Christians, I urge you in the strongest possible way: read this book! It is an urgently needed antidote to the toxic practices that are tearing our churches apart. Monique and Krista take on big, powerful, and complex ideas in clear, concise, and deeply biblical prose. Their humility, grace, humor, boldness, and courage shine on every page."

—**Scott D. Allen,** president, Disciple Nations Alliance, author of *Why Social Justice Is Not Biblical Justice: An Urgent Appeal to Fellow Christians in a Time of Social Crisis*

WALKING

IN

UNITY

KRISTA BONTRAGER
& MONIQUE DUSON

HARVEST HOUSE PUBLISHERS
EUGENE, OREGON

For bulk, special sales, or ministry purchases, please call 1-800-547-8979. Email: CustomerService@hhpbooks.com

Italicized emphasis in Scripture added by authors.

Cover design by Faceout Studio, Molly von Borstel

Cover images © Inhabitant B / Shutterstock

Interior design by KUHN Design Group

Interior illustrations on pages 71, 73, and 89 © Abigail Bontrager

The chart on page 75 is taken from Neil Shenvi and Pat Sawyer, *Critical Dilemma* (Eugene, OR: Harvest House Publishers, 2023), 96. Used with permission.

Walking in Unity
Copyright © 2024 by Krista Bontrager and Chantal Monique Duson
Published by Harvest House Publishers
Eugene, Oregon 97408
www.harvesthousepublishers.com

ISBN 978-0-7369-9089-9 (pbk)
ISBN 978-0-7369-9090-5 (eBook)

Library of Congress Control Number: 2024931374

Printed in the United States of America

24 25 26 27 28 29 30 31 32 / BP / 10 9 8 7 6 5 4 3 2 1

FROM MONIQUE

To my mom, Pauline, your wisdom has been a gift.
Thank you for teaching me how to fight.
To my siblings (by birth and by marriage)
and nephews…y'all the bomb-diggity!
To Krista and my Bontrager family, thanks for standing
with me and praying for me in my most difficult seasons.
I am deeply grateful for your love and adoption.

FROM KRISTA

To my mother, Bob, Emily, and Abigail,
thank you for cheering us on.
More than anyone else, you were the eyewitnesses
to the pain and joys of this journey,
You are just as much a part of the story as we are.
To Laura, thank you for being "the one" who
stayed and walked with us through these years.

CONTENTS

FOREWORD

Alisa Childers

T hroughout the summer of 2020, I had a knot in the pit of my stomach.

After the death of George Floyd on May 25, my social-media news-feed was inundated with black squares bearing the hashtags #blackouttuesday and #blacklivesmatter. Some of my white friends posted the black square with captions articulating that they had finally been awakened to the plight of black and brown people. Other white friends expressed sorrow and anger over Floyd's death but refrained from posting the hashtag or square. Still others carried on as if nothing had happened. Some of my black friends became very vocal about their belief that our country is racist and even challenged me privately to speak out against systemic racism. Other black friends shared heartbreaking stories of their personal experiences with racism. The pressure to post that square was intense, and the weight of expectations was heavy as a boulder. I froze. Although I was grieved by the tragedy, something didn't seem right. I wanted to comment on current events from a biblical perspective but felt a bit unmoored within the conversation.

Then my friend Krista Bontrager suggested I interview her friend Monique Duson on my podcast to talk about it. To put it lightly, I was nervous. I wanted to bring light and clarity to a divisive issue, but I didn't want to say the wrong thing. Culture was screaming that, as a white woman, all I could do was shut up, listen, and not offer an opinion. Yet the Bible says that what God says about human beings is true no matter what our sex or skin color. But given the social unrest, interviewing a black woman I had never met was intimidating. We recorded a full hour, and Krista, who was watching from the sidelines, popped in and said, "Well. That was the polite version. Why don't you try a prophetic version?"

Something clicked, and I thought, *Okay, let's do this.*

After a quick burger break, I scrapped the first conversation, and we recorded the episode that is now published on my podcast. The Center for Biblical Unity soon became one of the most trusted sources to help Christians navigate the chaos of 2020. But other voices were offering very different solutions.

The church is divided. The twin frameworks of black liberation theology and critical race theory have infiltrated even the most theologically conservative churches. Even congregations that would eschew progressive Christianity as a false gospel, shun the prosperity gospel as heresy, and reject deconstruction as a destructive path have been influenced by these frameworks in their discussions about race. Many well-meaning churches desperately want to recognize the sins of the past, root out racism, and engage in racial reconciliation. But as of now, there is one dominant model for achieving those goals—and sadly, it only leads to more confusion, division, and suspicion.

In *Walking in Unity*, Duson and Bontrager propose a new model—a biblical solution that defines terms, wrestles with difficult questions surrounding ethnicity, acknowledges the turbulent history of racism in our nation, and ultimately, helps Christians live out the reconciliation Jesus accomplished on the cross. It is my great hope that every church will read this book as a congregation and use it as a guide to have better discussions on race that are informed by the Scriptures and lived out with honesty and authenticity.

There's no shortage of books on race. There's no shortage of books on critical race theory or wokeness. But there's no other book like this one.

Duson and Bontrager have risen above the noise to provide the body of Christ with a practical resource that doesn't just teach ideas and concepts. It lifts the lid off their own personal journey of friendship and invites the reader to join them as they wrestle through inflammatory topics like racial reconciliation, systemic injustice, the multiethnic church, corporate repentance, and reparations. Their story serves as a beautiful example of two sisters in Christ realizing that this identity is more important than any other. They practice what they preach and truly live out what they write about. I know this because they have adopted my family as their own.

—**Alisa Childers,** host of
The Alisa Childers Podcast,
a.k.a. "The Aunty"

FINDING FRIENDSHIP

M onique and I (Krista) met in the fall of 2017. Little did we know that first meeting would mark the beginning of a long, uphill, but rewarding journey.

We met through a mutual friend, and for the first seven months, we conversed through Zoom and Facebook since Monique was serving as a missionary in South Africa. We discovered we had a lot in common: We were both raised in Southern California by single mothers. We had both faced sizable challenges as children. We were both passionate about our faith. We both despised hypocrisy. And we were both working in ministry.

Despite all the similarities, we never thought we'd be in ministry together.

Seven months into our friendship, Monique flew back to the United States to visit family, and I drove more than an hour to pick her up from LAX. We met face-to-face for the first time on June 3, 2018, with a curbside hug. Days later, Monique was forced to make an emergency transition off the mission field, and my husband and I invited her to stay with our family for three months while she readjusted to life back in the United States.

This arrangement lasted nearly five years.

THE CLASH OF WORLDVIEWS

There were many days in the first years of our friendship when it felt like we were locked in a duel. It was going to be a fight to the finish over which person's view of Scripture would prevail. If we were going to remain friends, I (Krista) could see that one of us was going to have to make a major shift in our way of seeing the world.

Monique was 100 percent committed to the idea that all white people are racist and that I read the Bible through the lens of whiteness. And I was 100 percent committed to the idea that the most important thing about both of us was that we should pursue the truth of Scripture first and foremost.

These two frameworks were not compatible. But I was willing to shift my point of view. In fact, I would often tell Monique, "Persuade me to your position." But I would add this caveat: "Show me from Scripture used in context that you are correct." I wasn't willing to simply throw away my worldview without a solid biblical warrant.

That's not to say I was always secure in my position. I was going against what the culture was screaming at me. Here I was, a white woman trying to tell a black woman that her theology was wrong and that I thought she was prioritizing her race over her identity in Christ. The dread and thoughts of insecurity flooded me at times, especially at night. *Am I just trying to be some kind of white savior? What if my way of reading the Bible is actually racist? Maybe I really am racist simply because I'm white.*

I started to frantically research everything I could about race, racism, and historical injustices. But I had to do this often in secret, usually at night after everyone else was asleep. Many nights I woke up in a panic, wondering if my strong stand for historic Christianity really was the right path to continue to take.

During this season, I also reached out to a few strangers on Twitter who are Christians and had come out of the social justice framework that Monique so strongly advocated for. I remember writing to one of them after Monique and I had a particularly bad argument. She encouraged me to stay the course and keep praying that the Lord would bring about a change in Monique's heart.

As it turned out, she was exactly right. Any changes Monique went through were because of supernatural situations orchestrated by the Lord. My methods of persuasion were no match for what the Lord would do.

NOT BRAINWASHED

Since starting the Center for Biblical Unity, some people have suggested that I (Monique) have been "brainwashed by the white woman." That was one leader's direct accusation. My response to these claims is always the same: "It's unfortunate that the attitude of your heart apparently does not allow for a black woman to change her mind or think for herself." Sometimes, you answer a fool according to their folly (Proverbs 26:4-5). Because I have not been brainwashed by Krista. On the contrary, I have been blessed by Krista.

I am my mother's stubborn child. When I was a teenager, her invitations for me to consider things differently always ended with her saying, "Kiki (my childhood nickname), I'm only asking you to bend, not break." I would rather break than bend on what I thought I was right about.

My attitude toward Krista was no different. Her questions and invitations for consideration only caused me to want to stand my ground more. My perspective was *not* going to change simply because I got tired and gave in or because Krista finally wore me down. I was too stubborn for that.

If my mind was going to change on the issues of race and social justice, it would be because God Himself showed me something different, something better. And He has! In my season of debate with

Krista, I took the route of searching out every well-loved Bible verse I knew to defend the Christian's responsibility to do social justice. But instead of only reading the verse, I read the whole book—of Micah, all of Luke, all of Amos—and I also read the books that Krista recommended: Ephesians, Exodus, Deuteronomy, and more.

As I looked deeper into Scripture, I realized two things. First, I had never taken time to read Scripture in context. I cherry picked the verses that were "deep" and "good" and meant something to me or the specific situation I was in. And, second, Krista knew a lot more than I did about exegeting texts. I had things to learn. It didn't make me bad, but it did make me wrong. And I would have to learn to humble myself if I wanted to truly understand God's heart for justice.

God did *not* put Krista in my life to show up as my "white savior," saving me from my "blackness" and bringing me into her kingdom of white. Instead, He used her to show up as a friend who cared enough to challenge me on my theology, regardless of the fact that I am black and she is white. God chose her to confront me on some very difficult topics, of which race and justice were just a few, but the way I viewed the world shifted as I grew in my understanding of the Scriptures. God speaks through His Word; as we listen and choose obedience, we must change.

THE CONFLICT

As you can tell, life under the same roof revealed that Krista and I had very different views of the world. The early years of our friendship were marked by many challenging, and often painful, discussions about race and racism. We were both filled with assumptions, accusations, hard words, and harder emotions. Sometimes this led to heated conversations and even needing to take a time-out, take a drive, and cool off.

Like many people in the United States today, we faced what felt like insurmountable barriers—while we spoke the same language, we had drastically different definitions for words related to race and racial issues. We also entered our friendship with cultural rifts that made talking about racial issues at times confusing and distressing. Instead of retreating permanently into avoidant silence or escalating until we burned down the friendship, we learned to enter those difficult conversations with more grace and humility because the other person was worth it.

You could say that because we lived in the same house, we were forced to find a way to preserve our friendship. We had a spoken agreement to choose the other person, even when we preferred not to. We deliberately kept the fun alive in our friendship and created happy memories together between the hard conversations. We also dove deeper into studying the Bible, seeking God's truth about the issues that divided us. And slowly, as we meditated on and discussed God's Word together, we both began to change.

WALKING TOGETHER

When I (Monique) returned from the mission field, I was diagnosed with post-traumatic stress disorder. As part of my recovery process, my therapist recommended going on daily walks, and Krista thought it would be great if she came with me. So every morning before Krista went to work, we walked three laps around our gated community, reaching two miles exactly. After work, we'd walk the same route again. Sometimes I'd even meet her at work in the middle of the day, and we'd take a quick walk during her lunch break. We walked so much that it felt like we covered the nearly ten thousand miles back to Cape Town.

On one of our first walks I asked, "So, are you a Republican?" Her face registered shock and confusion at my unsolicited inquiry. Since she didn't immediately respond with a hearty, "No way!" (or with any words at all, for that matter), I just kept talking.

"Republicans don't care about the poor. What are your thoughts on helping the poor?"

Krista remained silent, so naturally, I kept talking.

Finally, she spoke up. "I do care about helping the poor," she said. "But I also think I have different ideas than you do about *how* to do it. I don't really think I'm ready to share my political thoughts."

What? The only thing worse than a completely silent walk is one filled with mind-numbing small talk. If we were going to be real friends, we couldn't be "small-talk friends." I'm just not that type. I kept asking questions—not to bother her, but because I genuinely wanted to get to know her.

Our walks also gave Krista the opportunity to get to know me. She fumbled through her own questions at first, unsure of what was okay to ask and what would be considered rude or racist. But once she found her conversational stride, our walks turned into marathons of questions—very direct questions.

Krista asked me about things that had never crossed my mind— from my worldview and why I believed all white people were racists to why I wasn't married. She asked why I was okay with premarital sex in light of being a Christian. I tried to explain that I wasn't okay with *premeditated* premarital sex, but if you got caught up in the heat of the moment, and it accidentally happened, certainly God would extend grace. For every question she had challenging my errant views of Scripture, I had an answer. She wanted to know why I was so passionate about social justice and where I got the idea that Jesus was a social worker. (She especially disliked that one.)

"What was your experience like at Biola University?" she asked. (Like putting Snoop Dogg on *The Brady Bunch*.)

"Why did you vote for Obama?" (Because he was black, that's why!)

This question got us talking about identity politics and how I, as a Christian, could choose to vote for Democrats.

"Do all black people think like you?" she asked. Not about everything, necessarily, I told her, but about race, the police, and Democrats, definitely!

Krista continued,

"What's your family like?"

"What were the Los Angeles riots like?"

"What was your neighborhood like?"

Her strategically timed and direct questions kept me thinking.

Sometimes our conversations spilled over from our walks into the house. Krista was genuinely curious about black people and our culture. She often mistook the preferences of one black person as universal to black culture. I was curious too, but that interest extended only to Krista as an individual. Because I had been raised in a majority white nation, attended a predominantly white university, and worked among many white people, I thought I already knew everything I needed to know about white culture.

For example, I *knew* that, for white people, being too loud was nearly synonymous with being irreverent. And yet, white children always seemed a bit rowdier than what black mothers allowed from their own children. I *knew* all whites voted Republican and didn't seem to care too much about blacks or other minorities. They expected people of color to pull ourselves up by our bootstraps, clearly without any understanding of the historic racial injustice black people had suffered that had removed those boots altogether. I *thought* I knew plenty about what it meant to be white.

After a deeper study on race and Scripture, I realized I was wrong. I had lots of assumptions but not many facts.

Our conversations were lively, at best. At worst, they were heated arguments, ending with us in tears, walking away from each other, or not speaking to each other because our hot heads needed time to cool off. I was committed to my beliefs about racism, America's racist past, my thoughts on white people, and how Scripture should be lived out in light of those things. Meanwhile, Krista was committed to a historic Christian worldview and approach to Scripture. This is not to say that she didn't care about history or racism or injustice; she simply thought that to think correctly about those things, one first had to properly understand the Scriptures in context. This was a confusing idea for me, so I considered it another facet of whiteness. Nevertheless, we continued to walk.

We walked in summer and in winter. We didn't let changing seasons or the elements stop us. There were many times when neither of us wanted to show up because the relationship felt too hard. But we both knew that walking was healthy for me, and though we couldn't see it then, walking was healthy for our unity. That season of walking formed our friendship.

The conversations that flowed from those walks were a key part of what moved me away from the social justice ideology that had served as the framework for my worldview, and they also broadened Krista's understanding regarding issues of race and racism. Those conversations serve as the foundation for the Center for Biblical Unity and this book.

BEGINNING THE JOURNEY

In October 2019, I (Monique) made a YouTube video explaining changes in my thinking on race issues and who was actually my spiritual family. I called on all Christians, regardless of race, to treat one another first and foremost as family. Soon after this, the Lord planted in my mind the name for our ministry: the Center for Biblical Unity.

Despite not quite knowing what it would be, the following January, I filed paperwork for our organization to become a nonprofit. Krista built a four-page website for me, and in February 2020, the Center for Biblical Unity (CFBU) was born.[1]

We didn't have any solid plans for CFBU, but God did. When social unrest erupted in the late spring and summer of 2020, CFBU was positioned to offer a biblical voice on race, justice, and unity. God had placed us in the right place at the right time to speak truth into the chaos and proclaim His plan for racial unity.

Together we have had the privilege to travel across the country speaking on race, ethnicity, and culture. People have a lot of questions, and answering them can be complicated. Krista often compares this difficult undertaking to trying to solve a Rubik's Cube with forty-five sides. While we can't cover all forty-five sides of the race conversation in this brief book, we will answer the main questions we've received in our ministry. To maintain balance between our perspectives and approaches, you'll see that we've split the chapters roughly in half between us.

Along the way, we will examine how the *racial reconciliation* model and the *biblical unity* model address these race-related questions, and we will do our best to point you to the greatest healer and reconciler of all: Jesus. It is important to note that this book is not an academic response to critical race theory (CRT). Other authors have already done that work. We simply hope to equip regular Christians, including laypeople, pastors, Christian schoolteachers and administrators, and other ministry leaders to stand as countercultural voices and proclaim God's vision for biblical unity.

Because we are Christians, we ground our beliefs about race, racism, and justice in the tenets of Scripture. We also give strong deference to what Christianity has historically believed on these matters. It serves as our authority and the lens through which we see and make sense of the world. We believe that the Bible offers the best under-standing of human nature and the way the world really works. The available evidence combined with the work of scholars and Christian apologists have established that the words of the Bible are accurately preserved. We believe that the Bible is objectively true, regardless of whether a person believes or agrees with its teachings. As such, we have an obligation to conform our thoughts, feelings, and opinions to the Bible's directives. Because it is our authority, our primary desire is to explain what the Bible says before presenting our thoughts or opin-ions. If the Bible speaks clearly to a matter, we will say as much. If not, we will offer our perspective drawn from biblical principles and the best available evidence. We recognize that some of those opin-ions are debated points and may change over time.

We invite you to walk with us as we seek to conform our thoughts, feelings, and opinions on race, ethnicity, and culture to God's Word and His vision for unity. We pray that God will use the journey of our friendship to help you see the beautiful simplicity of His plan for racial unity: *family*.

May this book inspire you to boldly proclaim the hope God offers for racial unity—a better hope than *anything* the world has to offer.

CHAPTER 1

HOW DID WE BECOME SO DIVIDED?

Monique Duson

I grew up in South Central Los Angeles. Life was tough. But more than that, life was *black*. Lessons the streets taught me about drugs, prostitution, gangs, and being poor were secondary to what my mother instilled in me—being black. I was a black child and one day would grow up to become a strong, black woman.

My mother always based her most important life lessons on my blackness. For instance, when she wanted to remind me to think for myself, she'd say, "Kiki (my childhood nickname), you don't have to do what your little friends tell you to do—you hear me? The only two things you have to do in this world are be black and die."

Occasionally, we'd ride the bus to the Fox Hills mall. It was the bougie mall where "fancy" blacks and white people shopped. When we saw white kids throwing tantrums, my mother would remind my brother and me, "You see that? That's what white kids do. You better not ever!" And, just in case one of us was considering "acting a fool" in front of a white audience, she'd give us the pep talk, "Don't y'all get in here and start acting a fool in front of all these white people. You hear me?" ("Yes, ma'am" was the only appropriate response.) My mother listened to black music, so I listened to black music.

Her record player only turned for black singers: Regina Belle, Anita
Baker, Michael Jackson, Luther Vandross, Whitney Houston, Karyn
White, Prince, Sade, Stevie Wonder. The one and only time I listened
to "white music" while living at home was when I played Michael
Bolton, and all my mother said was, "That sounds like white music."
I immediately knew not to play it again.

It wasn't merely that there was something different about "white
music." I learned from an early age that black and white people were
different entirely. Race was an identity, not simply an aesthetic. Being
black was intrinsically who I was—not just how I looked.

MY GREAT AWOKENING

On April 29, 1992, I stood on the corner of 61st Street and Nor-
mandie Avenue in South Central Los Angeles and watched my
neighborhood burn. The previous year, Rodney King (a black man)
had been nearly beaten to death after being pulled over by four
(white) Los Angeles police officers after an eight-mile car chase.[1]
The whole thing, including the beating, was captured on video.
The recording proved to the world something the black community already *knew*: the system was stacked against us. The subsequent acquittal of all four officers resulted in riots that ripped the
city apart. While most of America watched the televised riots from
the safety of their living rooms, my family and I watched it from
right outside our home.

The year leading up to that moment had been a racially tumul-
tuous one for black people in South Central. In March 1991—just
13 days after King's beating—a Korean store owner shot a 15-year-
old black girl, Latasha Harlins, in the back of the head after wrongly
accusing her of trying to steal a bottle of orange juice.[2] This happened
three miles from my house. That November, Judge Joyce Karlin, who

was white, fined the store owner five hundred dollars and placed her on five years' probation. Residents of South Central were outraged and called for Karlin's removal.[3]

By the time the Rodney King trial ended five months later, the city was a racial tinderbox, primed to catch fire—and it literally did. Crowds ran down the street. Some people held protest signs and yelled, "No justice, no peace!" Looters carried off televisions, stereos, and clothes, targeting stores that were owned by Koreans or white people. Parents sent their kids to grab whatever they could. (My friends brought home 40-ounce liquor bottles for their father.)

My mother wouldn't let me or my siblings out of her sight. Finally, when I asked her what was going on, she said, "Kiki, white folks think they can do black people any kinda way. And we're tired. Black people are tired."

Until then, I hadn't really thought about the ways white people treated us. At this point in my life, all I knew about black-white relationships I had learned in school or by eavesdropping on my mother's conversations with her friends. I often heard her say, "White folks always gonna think they better than black folks."

Black people and white people were from two different worlds with little overlap. From what I could see, black folks lived in South Central and white people lived everywhere else. Any kid whose family left South Central to live somewhere else we labeled as "sadiddy," "uppity," or "acting white." We lived, shopped, went to school, and worshipped with people who looked like us, and white people did the same. I only had one white teacher throughout my entire elementary education, and we made fun of her.

My world wasn't so much filled with an understanding of racism as it was filled with the understanding that black and white people were different. Our differences meant we didn't interact on any level—no white friends, no white teachers, no white store owners.

My world was proudly black. "White" was reserved for my grandmother's soap operas, doctors, and folks you saw at work. Otherwise, we all kept to ourselves.

Division didn't start in 1992 with the Los Angeles Riots. We'd already been divided; I was just waking up to it.

AMERICA WAKES UP

Twenty-eight years later, inner-city Los Angeles was burning again, and this time, so were other black neighborhoods in cities across the country. This unrest was sparked by the death of George Floyd, a black man, who died while being detained by a white police officer in Minneapolis, Minnesota. The scenes were all too familiar—looting, burning buildings, and black rage. The screams of "No justice, no peace!" were now replaced with "black lives matter!" Celebrities and corporations denounced systemic racism and demanded that everyone recognize the racial injustices being committed against black people. The footage of Floyd pinned under the knee of Derek Chauvin, a white police officer was, for some, all the evidence needed to condemn America as a racist nation.

Until this uproar, most white people thought America had come a long way in race relations. Civil rights for all had been codified into law decades earlier. Interracial relationships were more widely accepted. Eminem, a white rapper, was accepted as a legit hip-hop artist in a space that had been completely black. And finally, for a brief moment, the television show *Friends* had a significant black character with a recurring role. Surely, America was headed toward a postracial society. There were black movies and television shows. A few *Fortune* 500 companies had black CEOs. Black people were working in STEM fields and nonprofit sectors. We'd elected America's first black president—*twice*. For many white people, this was evidence that America had put racism behind us. In light of what seemed like progress, the events of 2020 caught many off guard.

Most black Americans were not surprised, though. Conversations about race and injustice were still the waters that many black people were swimming in, and those waters ran deep. While many white people saw Floyd's death as the first recent sign of *potential* racism, many black people saw it as the last straw, the confirmation of long-standing systemic police bias against us. Between 2014 and 2020, several high-profile cases of black people being killed by the police had made headlines nationwide: Michael Brown, Eric Garner, Freddie Gray, Philando Castile, Alton Sterling, Botham Jean, Atatiana Jefferson, and Breonna Taylor among them. Many (but not all) of the offending police officers were white.

While much of 2020's social unrest mirrored 1992's, something was drastically different this time around—*me*. Through God's grace and many hard conversations with Krista (beginning in 2017) and divinely placed situations, I had been shifting away from the progressive social justice mindset I had adopted as a child. I started to ask different questions and became slower to jump to conclusions about people based on their skin color. I was now consulting Scripture as my first authority on issues of race, justice, and unity. As mentioned earlier, Krista and I started the Center for Biblical Unity (CFBU) in February 2020, just as rumors of the pandemic were surfacing. During the riots that summer, our ministry's popularity began to grow. As social media began focusing on "lifting black voices," my black voice was pushed out to hundreds of thousands of people every week.

But all of that stopped when the social-media algorithms realized I was a *theologically conservative* black voice, promoting a *biblical* path to racial unity. Once they caught on, they stopped promoting my black voice. (Perhaps their slogan should have been, "Lift *some* black voices.")

Nonetheless, in those early months, thousands of emails from, what was at the time, our mostly white audience poured in to CFBU, asking variations of the same question: *How did we become so divided?*

A PEOPLE DIVIDED

Complex questions call for careful answers. We kept hearing the same question: "How did we become so divided?" On the surface, the question was about United States history and slavery, Jim Crow, or civil rights. The underlying question, though, was much more complicated. Those who believed our nation was on a trajectory to a "post-racial" society wanted to know, "How could the death of George Floyd stop all our progress?" Christians specifically wondered:

"Why are our churches so divided?"

"What started the black church?"

"If we're all believers, why don't black and white people usually worship together?"

"What can we as Christians do to help heal racial division?"

Answering these questions and exploring every causative factor in detail would take a book of its own. Since much has already been written on the topic, I'll give an overview of four main factors of the division: nation, church, history, and culture.

Divided Nation

It is sobering to look back on our nation's history and remember that United States legal institutions once sanctioned the enslavement of black and indigenous Americans and allowed legalized discrimination to continue for more than one hundred years after the signing of the Emancipation Proclamation. While slavery dates back to some of the oldest civilizations and is mentioned in Genesis 37:2-36, slavery was seen as a result of fallen human nature and belonged to all people.[4] Although slavery was normal in most parts of the world throughout history, America pioneered a new version of it, which was predominantly based on skin color. This and other institutionalized racial mistreatment created its own kind of division in our nation, leading some to justify brutality toward (and even murder of) black people.[5]

Some Christians even argued that this was God's will because Africans descended from the line of Ham (Genesis 9:20-27). Since Noah had cursed Ham's son Canaan to be a "servant of servants" to his brothers, slavery advocates concluded this was a biblical war rant to enslave Africans. This view was published in books, pamphlets, sermons, and newspapers. Even Dr. Louis T. Talbot, namesake of Biola University's Talbot School of Theology, affirmed this interpretation as late as the 1940s. In a leaflet titled "Studies in Genesis" he wrote:

> But not only did the Canaanites prove to be morally and spiritually depraved and degraded. Not only was their immorality accompanied by the worst forms of idolatry. But they also became "abject slaves," servants of the descendants of Shem and Japheth.[6]

And yet again, certain historians tell us that, when Israel took the land, some of the Canaanites "fled away into Africa." Surely this curse upon Canaan gives us the only true account of the origin of the Negro race, "a servant of servants."[7]

Some also argued, then and more recently, that Africans descended from Adam's son Cain. After Cain killed his brother, Abel, God cursed him. But He also showed Cain mercy by putting a mark on him so he wouldn't be killed by others (Genesis 4:1-16). Although the Bible doesn't indicate what the mark was or whether it was passed down through Cain's descendants, some Christians thought that white skin was "normal" and interpreted the "mark" placed on Cain and his descendants as black skin.[8] Therefore, slavery, discrimination, bans on interracial dating and marriage, and other injustices were not only legislated, but *scripturally* justified. The dehumanization of black people resulted in inexcusable acts like the nonconsensual, forced obstetrics experiments performed without anesthesia on black slave women.[9] The publication of Charles Darwin's *Origin of the Species* (1859) and *Descent of Man* (1871) furthered these ideas and played a role in laying the scientific and philosophical groundwork used to justify future ideas like eugenics.

Divided Pews

When I was a child, my grandmother took me to Sardis Missionary Baptist Church—a black church that met in a small storefront building. There I learned to clap, shout, and sing old black worship songs like "Jesus Is on the Mainline." Some of the older women wore nursing uniforms and white gloves. These church "nurses" would catch kids or glasses when parents started to "shout" (which is church dancing, not random screaming). They'd also cover the legs of women lying on the floor after being slain in the Holy Ghost; this was to respect their modesty. Ushers (who would snatch the gum right out your mouth if they caught you chewing any!) seated attendees. The small choir marched in from the back of the sanctuary, their rhythmic sways and sharp turns commanding the attention of those in the pews. Musicians would beat on the Hammond organ and drums when the pastor was "preaching good," and "the mothers" (the oldest women in the church) would wave fans with pictures of Jesus on the front and a picture of Martin Luther King Jr. or funeral home advertisements on the back. (In the absence of air conditioning, these fans would be used to cool off, encourage the pastor, or fan people who passed out from "catching the Holy Ghost.")

That was all I knew about church.

I was my grandmother's church buddy. From the time I was a toddler, my grandmother would dress me up and take me to church with her, sometimes for multiple services. She was a diabetic and became very ill when I was ten, and she was no longer able to take me to church. Off and on her church friends would pick me up for Sunday service, but in the long run, her absence would result in me leaving the church. My grandmother died when I was 13. At that time, I had no personal faith or understanding of who Jesus or the Trinity was. Thankfully, a short three years later, a friend from my high school would invite me to her youth group at a large multiethnic church. There I would hear the gospel and choose to place my hope and trust in Jesus. Ten years passed before I returned to the black church. By then, I was studying at Biola University, a predominantly white Christian school in the Los Angeles Basin, when black friends invited me to a black church in Compton. I grew to love that community. The people took Christianity—and blackness—very seriously. This time around, the black church taught me what it meant to be a black Christian.

At Biola, I saw the stark difference between the black and white church. Collective worship at Biola usually meant slow music led by barefoot white people with guitars. There wasn't a whole lot of clapping (even less clapping on beat), and I barely knew any of the songs. I was out of my element. Occasionally, the university's gospel choir would be scheduled to sing black gospel music during the chapel service. Not everyone appreciated it, and some students asked why a gospel choir was even needed. The black and white church remained divided on that campus.

In a 1960 *Meet the Press* interview, Martin Luther King Jr. called eleven o'clock on Sunday mornings the most segregated hour in America.[10] While routine necessities of weekday life pushed white and black people into shared spaces at work and on public transportation, church services remained separate. Attending church with those of the same color and culture was standard and, in fact, preferred. While many within the black church fought for the civil rights reforms of the 1960s, most white evangelical churches appeared to remain silent on those issues. White evangelicals usually fell into one of three camps: segregationists (those wholly opposed to integration), moderates (who believed segregation to be biblically and legally wrong but frowned upon miscegenation [reproduction between people of different ethnic groups]), or integrationists (those who believed segregation was a sin and openly spoke against it on all levels).

Most white evangelical churches in both the North and the South were not completely silent on matters of racism. Many evangelical leaders openly condemned racism in their writings instead of joining black people marching in the streets.[11] While Dr. King and other civil rights movement leaders called for the government to address racism and segregation structurally, white evangelicals were largely of the mind that involving government was wrong. They believed that the end of racism would come, and it would be better accomplished by the gospel transforming individuals' hearts.[12] This notion added to the mistrust between black and white believers—a suspicion that continues today. Some black Christians still view all or predominantly white church congregations as racist or unsafe spaces.[13]

Segregation was standard in many churches from America's earliest days. White slave owners questioned whether black people could or should be offered the gospel and salvation. Christianity was seen as the religion of the free, and initially, slaves who accepted the gospel and were baptized were often freed. The Christian faith would not allow any Christian to own another,[14] but the Virginia slave law of 1667 began to change this practice nationwide by stating that "An act declaring that baptisme [sic] of slaves doth not exempt them from bondage." (White slaves who were baptized into Christianity, on the other hand, were freed afterward.)[15] Slave owners feared that teaching Christianity to their slaves would lead to revolts, escapes, or demands to be set free; therefore, they tightly controlled literacy, access to the Bible, and worship in the slave quarters. As a result, slaves created "invisible churches"—secret meetings where they could pray, worship, and listen to preaching without restriction.

Free blacks formed churches and held worship services, finding support from many white Methodists who generally welcomed both free and enslaved blacks. But even in this setting, racism eventually forced black and white congregants apart, leading to the formation of the black church.[16] This gave blacks a generally safe space to worship God through their own cultural expressions, though they still faced vandalism and bombings.

Sadly, an overemphasis on biblical themes of freedom from slavery, the Exodus, and God as the champion of the oppressed opened a door to reinterpret and reimagine Christianity through the experiences of oppressed people. James Cone, the father of black liberation theology, compared the black struggle for freedom from slavery to the Hebrews' exodus from Egypt and argued that God is, first and foremost, the God of the oppressed—therefore, white people can't possibly understand Him.[17] In one of his works, *Black Theology and Black Power* (1969), Cone writes,

> In Christ, God enters human affairs and takes sides with the oppressed. Their suffering becomes his; their despair, divine despair. Through Christ the poor man is offered freedom now to rebel against that which makes him other than human.[18]

Black liberation theology aims to liberate black people from white oppression while holding very strong—at times racist—views on what it means to be either black or white. It often conflates politics with theology and pits the "oppressed" against the "oppressor." God is seen primarily as the Liberator from earthly oppression rather than the Redeemer of sinners.[19]

Cone wasn't the first to hold this view—or the last. In 1895, African Methodist Episcopalian Bishop Henry McNeal Turner asked his congregants to see God in a new way, saying, "I worship a Negro God. I believe God is a Negro. Negroes should worship a God who is a Negro. If we are created in the image of God, then God is black."[20] Deeply influenced by leaders like Cone, Martin Luther King Jr., John Lewis, Reverend Al Sharpton, and Jesse Jackson, many black preachers still focus primarily on social justice messages pertaining to white-inflicted oppression.

Divided History

In history class at school, I learned about white-toward-black racism—slavery, lynching, water hoses, poll taxes, separate bathrooms and water fountains, and "Colored Only" signs. I thought these things were relics of the past.

My history teachers reinforced the beauty of my blackness. We were taught to be proud because, even though white people had tried to keep us down for centuries, black people were strong, smart, and talented. We weren't only slaves "beaten and mistreated for the work we gave."[21] That's only one small part of our history; our lineage was that of kings and queens. We were inventors and doctors, authors and poets, teachers and singers, and freedom fighters. My early days of studying black literature and authors like Maya Angelou taught me that despite our history, we rise.

To be black was to be phenomenal, and young black girls like me were being raised to be phenomenal black women. The story of my people was the story of rising, again and again, tired but determined, even while white people thought they could do us "any kinda way."

History is a divisive topic today, and many believe the idea, as I once did, that there is a white history and a black history of the United States. On my walks with Krista, this concept came up regularly. We each knew parts of American history—just not the same parts.

Once, Krista mentioned Benjamin Franklin. I enthusiastically responded, "Oh, wasn't he the fifth president?" Her silence and confused expression—and later, bursts of laughter—let me know I was wrong. Krista knew about the Declaration of Independence, the Constitution, the founding fathers, and the Bill of Rights. She knew all the words of the national anthem. I knew about the Emancipation Proclamation, Crispus Attucks, Juneteenth, Emmett Till, redlining, and Black Wall Street. I knew all the words of the Black National Anthem. Krista didn't even know there *was* a Black National Anthem. It's as if we had spent our childhoods learning about two different Americas.

Today, American history and how it is being taught has come under scrutiny. Over the years, intentional efforts have been made to educate the public on the historical contributions of black Americans. Carter G. Woodson began Black History Week (now expanded to Black History Month) in 1926 to increase knowledge of black people's contributions to American society.

But since then, new endeavors to revise American history have come to the forefront. For example, Nikole Hannah-Jones's 1619 Project "aims to reframe the country's history by placing the consequences of slavery and the contributions of black Americans at the very center of our national narrative."[22] But our nation's history doesn't and shouldn't belong to just one group. It's *all* American history—and we should all know about all of it. It should serve as a guide, leading us to live wisely by exposing the patterns of our successes and mistakes.

Sadly, some people are taught certain pieces of history, and others are taught entirely different pieces. The way history is taught often depends upon the teacher's proficiency or priorities. Leaving out any "side" is incomplete and unrealistic. Is the moon landing not part of my history because I am black and Neil Armstrong and Buzz Aldrin were white? Should the Emancipation Proclamation be considered white history because Lincoln was white? What are we to make of black slave owners like Anthony Johnson, Elizabeth Frazer Skelton, William Ellison, and John Carruthers Stanly?[23] Do they belong to black history or white? To categorize the work of Frederick Douglass, Charles Octavius Boothe, or Daniel Hale Williams as only black history and not American history simply because of their brown skin demeans their contributions to our nation and silos them into a much narrower, less significant category: race.

To omit or minimize one group to highlight another is dishonest to who we are as a nation. We must not rewrite our historical narrative to center the accounts of one group or minimize the harms many have endured. We must not teach only the good or only the bad. Yet too often, that is exactly what happens. To overcome racial divisions, we must tell a full and accurate history. A split history is no history at all.

Cultural Division

Culture demands that we divide. By "culture," I mean the values, behaviors, customs, and ideologies social-media influencers, newscasters, musicians, athletes, celebrities, academics, ideologues, and everyday people see as routine, acceptable, and beneficial. These values often strive against those of the historic Christian worldview.

During the unrest of 2020, people were going berserk on social media, demanding that everyone post black squares on their pages to show their support for black people. Many who didn't were publicly shamed. Businesses were targeted. Pastors publicly called for congregants to deny their privilege and support Black Lives Matter. The narrative was that all black people are systemically oppressed. Anyone who questioned that was labeled a racist.

Cultural divisions have also deepened due to widespread "diversity" practices in hiring and recruiting. It is now common for employers to favor a "candidate of color" or ignore other applicants because of race-based practices meant to bring about diversity.[24] Some see these practices as a necessary corrective to compensate for historic injustices and as a means to achieve "equity"; others see them as exchanging one form of discrimination for another.

HOW DID WE BECOME SO DIVIDED?

The answer to this question may differ according to whom you ask. Someone's worldview will likely determine how he or she identifies the origins of division today, both in the church and the culture, but most will look to American slavery as the starting point.

But I believe this is the wrong place to start. Before George Floyd, before Rodney King, and before slavery, were Adam and Eve. Our ethnic division, at its foundation, is rooted in the sin and division of humankind's first family (Genesis 3:1-7).

Racial division is a byproduct of sin, and that sin starts in the broken hearts and bent nature of human beings.

Our nation's past, church divisions, incomplete history, and secular cultural pressures certainly play a role in our division too. Adopting race as our core identity, ignoring or nursing unhealed wounds and distrust, and catalyzing events among racial groups also contribute to this brokenness. We may find an infinite number of explanations for modern racial division, but the heart of the issue is *sin*.

When God asked Adam and Eve why they had done the one thing He specifically told them not to do—thereby damaging for all time their perfect fellowship with Him and each other—the first man blamed his wife instead of confessing his disobedience and willful rebellion. The cycle of sin, blame, and division between people had begun. Something had gone very wrong. Sin brought with it severe consequences: breaking the relationship between God and His people, the unity between man and woman, and the harmony between humans and the rest of creation (Genesis 3:8-24). This strife between Adam and Eve continued down through their descendants.[25] Genesis 4 records Cain's jealousy-driven murder of his younger brother, Abel, and Lamech's vengeful murder of a young man who had only wounded him (Genesis 4:23-24). The rest of the Bible confirms that sin and strife have been passed down through every generation. All of humanity has been affected by the first humans' rebellion, and division is one aspect of it that we still participate in today.

Our biggest race problems are neither liberal policies nor conservative policies. I could easily criticize those who choose to not speak out against biblically defined injustice. Rather, the line we must draw is between Christianity and culture. Regardless of one's political or ideological affiliation, culture will always fail to bring about true unity. Any culture that is not rooted in Christ can only foster more division.

In 1992, I saw that reality up close as I stood beside my mother and watched my neighborhood burn. At the time, my mom didn't know Christ, so her immediate response was to blame white people for the looters' poor behavior. The biblical answer, though, is that all people are sinners, and sinners are going to sin.

So who is to blame for today's division? The answer, quite simply, is all of us.

REFLECTION QUESTIONS

1. From this chapter, what did you learn about the history of slavery and race relations that surprised you?

2. What conversations in your own life have led you to reexamine your perspectives on social or spiritual issues? What is the value of having relationships with people who challenge you?

3. What are some recent examples of racial division you've witnessed? How does understanding the sinfulness of human nature impact how you view these conflicts?

4. How does your faith inform how you perceive the politics surrounding race relations in the US? How does your personal background (cultural, racial, political, socioeconomic, and so on) inform how you see these issues?

5. How does a fuller understanding of Western and American history affect how you understand today's conflicts in the US? Are there any areas of history highlighted in this chapter that you'd like to examine further?

CHAPTER 2

HOW SHOULD CHRISTIANS THINK ABOUT RACIAL UNITY?

Monique Duson and Krista Bontrager

⬤

"If Monique ruled the world, how would you fix the racial tensions happening in so many churches?"

We were only 100 feet from the front door, but Krista saw just enough time to squeeze in one last question about race before we finished one of our daily walks.

I (Monique) responded, "Racial reconciliation." Until 2018, this was my answer to any Christian asking what needed to be done about racism. To those outside the faith, I commended the work of antiracism.

"Tell me more," Krista said.

I first heard the term *racial reconciliation* as a sophomore at Biola. At the time, my understanding was that this model aimed to get believers of different races together at a common "table" of fellowship to discuss the ways in which white people had mistreated people of color. This gathering would be a time to share our pain and have our experiences as minorities affirmed. No questions would be asked about whether the people to whom we expressed our grievances were responsible for our experiences or if they had resources to help alleviate our oppression. Because they were white and thus part of the systemic problem, they should be made aware of the ways people of color experienced white-to-black racism daily. Later, we could explain ways white people could better participate in ending oppression against black people. The greater goal was for white people to stand with the dispossessed—in heart, mind, and soul.[1] Anything less would not be true reconciliation. I believed the main scriptural warrant for this was found in the last half of 2 Corinthians 5:18, which says God "gave us the ministry of reconciliation." In my mind, that included racial reconciliation.

Confused, Krista simply said, "I don't think that verse means what you think it means."

This conversation simulates how many people in churches, Christian schools, and ministries often talk about race. Many well-meaning people of faith use the phrase "racial reconciliation" without understanding that there are two broad models floating around Christian circles to help bridge racial divides. Despite using similar terminology, the models, which are meant for analyzing and addressing race and racism, are not much alike. Krista represented one model; I represented the other. The long process of listening, asking questions, debating, and trying to understand each other's perspective helped us uncover the structures of these two contrasting models.

The model adopted by a church, ministry, or institution often sets the direction for how its people interact with one another. We will provide a brief overview of both models here and then expand these themes throughout the remainder of this book.

THE RACIAL RECONCILIATION MODEL

Within broader secular culture, racial reconciliation is often known as *antiracism*. This model emphasizes race, equity of outcomes, changing systems, and achieving reconciliation between groups by addressing historical wrongs and disparities. Well-known proponents of antiracism include Robin DiAngelo (author of *White Fragility*) and Ibram X. Kendi (author of *How to Be an Antiracist*). Principles from this line of thinking have become embedded into policies and practices in education, social services, adoption agencies, and *Fortune* 500 companies nationwide.

Within Christian circles, aspects of antiracism are used to promote "racial reconciliation." This approach is exemplified by leaders such as Latasha Morrison (author of *Be the Bridge*), the Jude 3 Project, and Jemar Tisby (who briefly worked for Kendi's Center for Antiracist Research in 2021 and is the author of *The Color of Compromise*). Many others within the church have absorbed and applied pieces of this model in different ways and to different degrees. Throughout the book, we will quote from advocates of the racial reconciliation model, but it should also be understood that there isn't complete agreement on every point throughout that camp. In general, however, racial reconciliation advocates agree on the following set of ideas.

● The main problem behind racial division is that large-scale systems of oppression, created by white people to hold back people of color, are embedded in America's past and present. While many of these systems have technically been dismantled, their continuing effects and the ongoing social systems of "whiteness" today perpetuate racial injustice. Among scholars, whiteness is defined as a dimension of racism, that serves to benefit white people and disenfranchise people of color through the normalization of white standards or customs, by which all other people or groups are compared.[2] In her 1993 book, *White Women, Race Matters*, Ruth Frankenberg puts it this way,

> Whiteness is a location of structural advantage, of race
> privilege. Second, it is a "standpoint," a place from which

white people look at ourselves, at others, and at society.
Think, "whiteness" refers to a set of cultural practices that
are usually unmarked and unnamed.[3]

When these academic definitions show up in the real world, their
implications can be very harmful and lump people into buckets simply based on their skin color. For example, in 2020, the Smithsonian,
the world's largest museum and research center posted this statement
on their website:

> Whiteness and white racialized identity refer to the way that
> white people, their customs, culture, and beliefs operate
> as the standard by which all other groups of are compared.
> Whiteness is also at the core of understanding race in
> America. Whiteness and the normalization of white racial
> identity throughout America's history have created a culture
> where nonwhite persons are seen as inferior or abnormal.[4]

Only when these systems have been eradicated will racism be
eradicated.

The remedy for racial tensions is to actively "do the work" of antiracism.[5] This means pursuing equity of results across racial groups,
lamenting past and present acts of perceived racism, repenting of
whiteness, "decolonizing" Christianity, and supporting policies such
as wealth redistribution and racial reparations.

Racial reconciliation, even within the church, can really only be
achieved when all racial groups reach a shared agreement about historic injustices and required remedies, and when white people understand their privilege within society, divest themselves of social power,

and work to amplify the voices of (certain) people of color and other marginalized groups. Those who do not acknowledge the problem and also participate in the solution, as outlined by the racial reconciliation model, are often seen as racist, or at least contributing to ongoing systems of racism.

Racial Reconciliation as Antiracism

As I (Monique) have read widely on the issues of antiracism and racial reconciliation, I've come to believe that, in most cases, racial reconciliation is antiracism with a few scriptures layered on top. The two frameworks are nearly identical in theory and in practice. Advocates of the biblical unity model (which we'll explain more about) and the racial reconciliation model both see racism as a sin issue. But after acknowledging racism as a sin, most racial reconciliation advocates bring in antiracist terms and definitions (based in the social sciences) that are largely concerned with disparities, structural policies, and power dynamics as both proof of, and remedy for, the sin of racism.

For example, let's consider the term *racism* itself.

As I was writing this chapter, I asked my mother how she would define racism without looking in the dictionary. She said it's "when a member or group of people from one race do not like members from another race because they believe their race is superior."

My mother's definition of racism reflects a view held by many people, especially older generations. Historically, racism has been defined as a belief in the superiority of one ethnic group over others, which may result in targeting specific people or groups through prejudice, discrimination, or violence. This was primarily an issue of an individual's sinful heart.

This definition of racism underwent a seismic shift in 1970 when academic psychologist Patricia Bidol-Padva, in her out-of-print booklet *Developing New Perspectives on Race*, proposed a new definition:

"prejudice plus power."[6] Bidol-Padva was among the first to connect racism to institutional power, writing:

> Racism is racial prejudice (the belief that ones own race is superior to another race) combined with the power to enforce this bias throughout the institutions and culture of a society. In our society white racial prejudices are reinforced by our institutions and culture because we whites presently control the decision making and standard setting processes within them. As a result, white-originated standards are normative, which leads to illegitimate privileges for whites, who are receiving benefits just because they are white, and subordination of blacks and other third world peoples, who are being oppressed because they are not white... Racism = Power + Prejudice.[7]

This shift in definition from the individual to institutional power dynamics pigeonholed white people into the role of racist oppressors, guilty (at least) by complicity. It also perpetuates the idea of black powerlessness and victimhood.

In a 2022 panel discussion hosted by *Christianity Today*, pastor and racial reconciliation advocate Derwin Gray, author of *How to Heal Our Racial Divide: What the Bible Says, and the First Christians Knew, about Racial Reconciliation*, defined racism as "a sin that dishonors God." Here we have a point of mutual understanding with Gray. But, in the same conversation, he continued:

> Racism also deals with structural power for the majority group. African Americans in America can be prejudiced, but we can't develop a racist society because we don't have the *political or majority power* to do so. So racism deals

more with a systemic structure where advantages are given to whoever the top group is.[8]

In the same discussion, Dr. Christina Edmondson, a Christian antiracism advocate and coauthor of *Faithful Antiracism*, confirms that the social sciences must be consulted when addressing the topic. She said,

> When we think about concepts and terms, we want to think about what disciplines they live within. When we think about something like race, racialization, or racism, we're looking largely at anthropology, sociology, the social sciences.[9]

Later she expanded the 1970s definition of racism, saying it's "the racial *prejudice plus the social power* to embed that stratification into policies, practices, philosophies, etc."[10]

These prominent Christian leaders seem to borrow language from Bidol-Padva. To varying degrees, they also sound a lot like popular secular voices in the current conversation. For example, bestselling author and "antiracism workshop facilitator"[11] Robin DiAngelo explains racism this way:

> When a racial group's collective prejudice is backed by the *power* of legal authority and *institutional* control, it is transformed into racism, a far-reaching *system* that functions independently from the intentions or self-images of individual actors...Racism—like sexism and other forms of oppression—occurs when a racial group's prejudice is backed by legal authority and institutional control. This authority and control transform individual

prejudices into a far-reaching system that no longer depends on the good intentions of individual actors; it becomes the default of the society and is reproduced automatically. Racism is a system.[12]

Beverly Daniel Tatum, author of the influential book *Why Do All the Black Kids Sit Together in the Cafeteria?* (which used to be my all-time favorite book), also defines *racism* within that framework.

Another related definition of racism, commonly used by antiracist educators and consultants is "prejudice plus power." Racial *prejudice*, when combined with *social power*—access to social, cultural, and economic resources and decision making—leads to the institutionalization of racist policies and practices.[13]

One final example is from Ibram X. Kendi, professor and author, whose book *How to Be an Antiracist* has arguably done more to shape the popular conversation on race in the last several years than anything else, concedes that while it's possible for black people to hold a limited amount of institutional power, the default setting for most institutions is built on white supremacy. "Racism," he writes, "is a powerful collection of racist policies that lead to racial inequity and are substantiated by racist ideas."[14]

Notice that both the Christian racial reconciliation advocates and the secular antiracists all use the same "prejudice plus power" definition of racism as their foundation. This is repeated as an unquestioned mantra, as are its related ideas: white people cannot be the victims of racism, people of color cannot be racist (only prejudiced), and racism is the ordinary, everyday experience of people of color due to pervasive racist policies and values. In *Beyond Racial Gridlock*,

George Yancey, a Christian sociologist and professor of sociology at Baylor University, writes:

> Christians latched onto these solutions and came up with the more spiritualized term "racial reconciliation." Our attempts at spiritualization are admirable, but they cannot hide the fact that we have generally taken secular concepts and given them a Christian makeover. We should avoid making the mistake of thinking that just because we have spiritualized a secular model, the model is any less incomplete.[15]

Because this book is directed toward a Christian audience, we will use the term *racial reconciliation* to describe the Christian version of antiracism. In doing so, we recognize that there will be minor differences concerning issues of race and racism depending on which voices are being consulted, but for the most part, we see these two frameworks as virtually synonymous in theory and practice.

In my (Monique) experience, these calls to racial reconciliation seem to lead to more division and separation. I think the racial reconciliation model contains several serious flaws: It fails to interpret key biblical texts accurately, takes the wrong starting point, and heaps undue burdens onto the shoulders of all Christians to "do the work" that only Christ can do. We believe the racial reconciliation model—influenced by antiracism—is failing the church. Studies indicate that antiracism models and practices may in fact increase negative impacts on minorities in the workplace. Research gathered from the Barna group in 2020 indicates that churchgoers have grown increasingly reluctant to address racial issues within their congregations since the racial reconciliation model's advent.[16]

We do not assume negative motives from those who hold to this model. For many years, it was the primary scaffolding for my work in social service and overseas missions; it appealed to my sense of compassion and desire to find justice for the poor and minorities, as it does for many. But we want to invite those drawn toward racial reconciliation to explore the Bible's better plan for unity and justice.

THE MODEL FOR BIBLICAL UNITY

Throughout this book, we'll lay out the application of what we call the *biblical unity model.* The foundation of this model is Scripture. That's not to say we don't consider extrabiblical data when discussing race or racism, but our priority is to first investigate what the Bible has to say about issues related to ethnicity and justice through the lens of redemptive history—namely creation, fall, redemption, and new creation.

The biblical unity model is built on four principles: creation identity, salvation identity, matters of providence, and walking in unity.

Principle 1: Creation Identity

While the word *identity* isn't in the Bible, we will use it as shorthand for God's objective declarations about humanity. Identity is a meaningful way of helping us think accurately about ourselves and others, according to the Word of God.

Human identity begins with creation. Our creation identity isn't just a nice idea that's true for some societies but not others. It is *the* foundational identity for *all* human beings in *all* times and *all* places, whether we overtly recognize it or not.

The early chapters of Genesis describe our origins and tell the story of how God, by His will and His word, shaped the physical world and us in it. These early chapters also reveal five major pillars that uphold the Christian view of what it means to be human.

PILLAR 1

God specially created the first humans, the
original ancestors of all human beings.

God gave unique attention to the formation of Adam and Eve (Genesis 1:26). He was directly involved in their creation (Genesis 2:7, 21). This first pair were real historical people (Luke 3:38; Romans 5:12, 14), the first parents of all humans (Genesis 3:20; Acts 17:26). Within Adam and Eve lay the possibility of all the ethnic diversity we see today.

PILLAR 2

God created both the man and the woman in His image.

While both humans and animals were made from the dust of the ground (Genesis 2:7, 19), humans alone bear the *imago Dei* (image of God; Genesis 1:27) and the "breath of life" (Genesis 2:7). The psalmist describes humanity as being made "a little lower than the heavenly beings" (Psalm 8:5). The imago Dei is the source of human dignity. This means that all human beings—no matter where they live, who their parents are, whether they are Christians, or whether others see them as valuable—have inherent value, dignity, and worth. Nothing can change that.

PILLAR 3

God commanded humans to marry and procreate.

In creating Adam and Eve, God instituted the first family. Since the beginning, His design for human flourishing has been for people to grow up, marry one member of the opposite sex, bring children into the world, and remain together in loving commitment for life (Genesis 1:28; 2:24; 9:1). While God's plan for procreative "fruitfulness" has recently fallen from favor in Western society, His design for marriage and the family unit still stands as the best safeguard for human dignity and well-being. Societies thrive when God's design is honored. That is not to say that all (or any) marriages are perfect, nor that single adults or infertile couples have less inherent dignity than fertile, married couples. It simply means that God created human beings with purpose and instituted the marriage union (and through it, the family unit) for our good.

PILLAR 4

God appointed the man and
the woman to govern the earth.

God's original plan is revealed in His command for Adam and Eve, their children, and their children's children to work the ground (Genesis 2:15) and rule the earth (Genesis 1:26, 28). They were to expand the garden of Eden until they eventually brought the entire planet under their gracious stewardship. Human beings were made to participate in meaningful work, not avoid it.

PILLAR 5

Rebellion against God brought sin into the
world, affecting all aspects of life.

Rebellion meant work would become harder, pain in childbearing would increase, the relationship between human beings and the land would worsen, and Adam and Eve would no longer have the sanctuary of the garden of Eden (Genesis 3:23-24). They could no longer walk guiltlessly in God's presence. And the generations to come would witness, suffer from, and participate in the spread of evil.

These five pillars are God-determined realities, including what it means to be a human and not an animal, giving us our ultimate purpose in the new creation. The concepts of universal human rights *originate* from Genesis 1 through 3. Without the intrinsic worth endowed by our Creator, we have no philosophical ground for dignity, human rights, or moral obligation to act justly toward others. These are distinctly Christian ideas.[17]

Principle 2: Salvation Identity

Salvation identity is added to our creation identity: God created us and then redeemed us through Christ. It is grounded in four new realities that guide how we think and live as Christians.

REALITY 1

For those who are "in Christ," God is now our Father.

A common adage says, "The ground is level at the foot of the cross." The biblical unity model centers on the accomplished work of Christ instead of racial identity. On the cross, Jesus accomplished the work of achieving unity, which now opens up the possibility for all sinners, Jews and Gentiles alike, to become coheirs with Him. All are invited into a relationship with the Father through the work of the Son to become children of God (John 1:11-13; Ephesians 1:5; Romans 8:15), though only a few will come (Matthew 22:1-14). The foundation for unity is realized when people come into a relationship with the Father. For believers, unity is our starting point, not a destination to be achieved.

REALITY 2

Those who are "in Christ" are now part of a new spiritual family.

With God as our Father, it should come as no surprise that family language permeates the New Testament. Jesus's death and resurrection creates an objective new reality. As His disciples, we become spiritual brothers and sisters, fathers and mothers to one another (Matthew 12:46-50; 1 Timothy 5:1-2). So, while all humans are created in the image of God, not all humans are children of God. Salvation identity applies exclusively to those who are "in Christ."

REALITY 3

God's spiritual family is called out from every nation.

God is calling individuals from among the nations to become one new people (Revelation 5:9-10; 7:9). This new group of people is called the church. The Greek word *ekklesia* (translated "church" in English) literally means "called-out ones." The universal church has been ethnically and culturally diverse since Pentecost (Matthew 28:18-20; Acts 2:9-12) and has continued to expand to this day. An ethnically diverse body of Christ is a global reality even now.

REALITY 4

Our salvation identity enables us to live
out our creation identity in eternity.

Humans were originally created to reign over this creation and steward it on God's behalf (Genesis 1:26-27). Those who are in Christ will rule and reign with Him for all eternity (Revelation 20:6; 22:5).

When we put all the biblical evidence together, an important truth emerges: a natural outcome of becoming a true child of God is that we become members of a multiethnic, multicultural, inter-generational movement of God across thousands of years of history. In other words, we join a family. Unity is possible because Christians participate with each other from the position of brothers and sisters. Jesus has done all the work necessary to make cultural enemies into family. It's our job as His children to spread that good news.

Principle 3: Matters of Providence

"Would you consider yourself a black woman first? Or a Christian first?" We were 90 seconds away from starting a livestream when I (Krista) asked Monique that question. I immediately regretted blurting it out so carelessly as I watched tears come to her eyes.

Monique, like many in our culture today, was raised to think about identity hierarchies based on social categories, one of which is race. So my impulsive question unsettled her. Thankfully, God redeemed the situation: It sparked a journey for her to reconsider where she anchored her identity. This became a key turning point for her and the beginning of a two-year truth-seeking journey for us both. During that period, we began to explore what eventually we came to call "matters of providence"—the third principle of our biblical unity model.

Just as creation identity applies to all human beings, so do matters of providence. By *providence* we mean that God "governs all things according to the purpose of His will," and through His wisdom, cares for and directs all things in the universe, including the specific time and place into which we are born.[18] God cares about and is involved in the details of our lives, including ethnicity, national origin, family history and relationships, socioeconomic status, and more. His providence also means that He allows us to be born into tough situations, like fatherless homes or poverty. One of the mysteries of His will is that God doesn't always intervene or override the will of sinful humans. While we do not have control over these matters of providence, they often play an important role in our lives.

One of the issues that deserves more discussion between advocates of the two models involves how to categorize matters of providence in the hierarchy of identities. Should things like race, culture, and ethnicity be categorized as foundational to our identity (at the level of creation identity) or as secondary issues? When I hear racial reconciliation advocates use terms like *blackness* and *whiteness*, I'm often left wondering where those identities fall in relation to my creation identity and my salvation identity.

The biblical unity model categorizes creation identity and salvation identity as logically outranking matters of providence. Galatians 3:26-29 and Colossians 3:10-11 play a critical role in our understanding of this issue.

> In Christ Jesus you are all sons of God, through faith. For as many of you as were baptized into Christ have put on Christ. There is neither *Jew nor Greek, neither slave nor free, there is no male and female,* for you are all one in Christ Jesus. And if you are Christ's, then you are Abraham's offspring, heirs according to the promise (Galatians 3:26-29).

> [You] have put on the new self, which is being renewed in knowledge after the image of its Creator. Here there is no *Greek and Jew, circumcised and uncircumcised, barbarian, Scythian, slave, free;* but Christ is all, and in all (Colossians 3:10-11).

These verses reveal the interplay between our salvation identity, creation identity, and matters of providence. Whether we are male or female (creation identity), slave or free (a matter of providence), Jew, Gentile, barbarian, or Scythian (a matter of providence), our highest identity is that of belonging to Christ (salvation identity). The implications of this are important to consider. While a Christian man may be a slave in his everyday life, his character might qualify him to be an overseer in the church (1 Timothy 3:1-7; Titus 1:6-8). In fact, according to church tradition, Onesimus—the slave mentioned in Philemon—went on to become a bishop. Scythians were known in the ancient world for being nomadic warmongers. Being a barbarian was a way of referring to a non-Roman, who were all assumed to be uncivilized. In the first century, a local church could be filled with cultural enemies, with a Roman centurion sitting next to a Jew sitting next to a tax collector sitting next to a slave sitting next to a slave owner. But, in Christ, a more foundational reality emerges: family.

That's not to say Christians can't have a level of pride in our heritage or other matters of providence. The apostle Paul himself was vocal about the advantages of his heritage. But his tribal pride paled in comparison to his identity in Christ:

> But whatever gain I had, I counted as loss for the sake of Christ. For his sake I have suffered the loss of all things and *count them as rubbish*, in order that I may gain Christ and be found in him (Philippians 3:7-10).

The objective reality of our salvation identity, and the need to preach the gospel, reprioritizes matters of providence as secondary. In fact, Paul sets a strong example for us to pray for those who are in our ethnic or familial tribe, that they too would come to believe in Jesus as their Messiah (Romans 10:1-2).

The claim that our salvation identity is more foundational than matters of providence in the hierarchy of identities should not be used to erase the reality of the circumstances that we have been born into. Becoming a Christian doesn't wipe away all our challenging circumstances or a nation's rough history between ethnic groups. But for us Christians, those conversations must always be conducted with an eye toward the fact that there is a deeper truth about our salvation identities as individuals.

Because our family history, ethnicity, and cultural heritage fall under God's providence, we are free to embrace them as things He has granted to us. We can celebrate their beauty and our ancestors' pain and efforts to overcome adversity. We can also recognize their flaws. For some, celebrating God's providence might include preserving family or cultural customs, language, clothing, dance, music, recipes, or holidays. As long as traditions don't invite us to engage in non-Christian religious practices—such as ancestor worship or spiritism—or degrade our creation identity through immoral actions, we believe many issues of providence can be preserved and celebrated.

This framework gives someone like our friend Ryan Bomberger, who was conceived in rape (a matter of providence), inherent dignity from the moment of conception (creation identity) and the opportunity for a new identity as a child of God (salvation identity). As it happens, Ryan is biracial—so the fact that creation and salvation identities supersede matters of providence helps to settle confusion about which community he belongs to. This understanding also resulted in Monique investigating more about her family's origins a couple years ago. Many descendants of slaves have a very limited understanding about the deeper aspects of their family origins. Whether we find ourselves confronted with difficult or joyful aspects of matters of providence in our lives and relationships, Christians can keep them in proper perspective by remembering they are secondary to our salvation identity but still worthy of being explored, understood, and celebrated.

Principle 4: Walking in Unity

The biblical unity model does not deny historic racial injustice or turn a blind eye to it when we see it today. But the biblical unity model invites Christians to investigate how to live righteously in light of God's eternal moral law, including standing against racism as defined by Scripture. (We will spend an entire chapter summarizing our approach to this issue later.)

While the racial reconciliation model claims steps must be completed to achieve reconciliation between cultural enemies, the biblical unity model proceeds from a starting point of family. Instead of striving in human strength to accomplish what only God can, the biblical unity model starts with what Christ has *already* done through His work on the cross. Christians have a better hope for unity—one based on grace, not works. In this model, unity is our foundational starting point and identity, not a destination to be achieved. The Bible not only provides the proper standard for justice and guidance for how to live according to God's ways; it also offers a better hope for unity than anything the world has to offer. And we invite you into that better hope.

REFLECTION QUESTIONS

1. How can you move forward in a relationship with someone when you fundamentally disagree on a core issue? Are there situations where this is impossible?

2. How has this chapter's perspective on identity challenged your current definition of identity?

3. In your own life, how have you experienced conversations about antiracism and racial reconciliation? How have you seen these conversations arise in the church and your Christian community? What are the good and bad fruits of these beliefs?

4. How does understanding the Bible affect how you understand your own identity? How does the concept of "creation identity" contrast with culture's definition of identity?

5. How does the cross unify Christians? How should this unity determine how you view race-related cultural concerns?

CHAPTER 3

WHAT DOES THE BIBLE HAVE TO SAY ABOUT RACE?

Krista Bontrager

⬤

You know race is a social construct, right?"

Monique said it so confidently, taking for granted that I would understand.

She continued, "Race is made up. It's fake." As usual, I was rushing to catch up. I had a feeling that this walk was going to include a tough conversation.

Up to that moment, I had given about three seconds of thought to what it means to be a "white person." I quickly clapped back: "I'm white. You're black. It doesn't look made up to me."

Monique's frustration at my ignorance and flippancy was unmistakable. So I did what I always do: research. I began with something basic—the dictionary. Here's how *Merriam-Webster* defines race:

> Noun. any one of the groups that humans are often divided into based on physical traits regarded as common among people of shared ancestry.[1]

Since humans are grouped according to physical traits—black, white, Asian, and so on—that definition seemed straightforward. The end. Simple. Then I read the footnote:

> This use of *race* dates to the late 18th century, and was for many years applied in scientific fields such as physical anthropology, with race differentiation being based on such qualities as skin color, hair form, head shape, and particular sets of cranial dimensions. Advances in the field of genetics in the late 20th century determined no biological basis for races in this sense of the word, as all humans alive today share 99.99% of their genetic material. For this reason, the concept of distinct human races today has little scientific standing, and is instead understood as primarily a sociological designation, identifying a group sharing some outward physical characteristics and some commonalities of culture and history.[2]

After reading this, an entirely different group of questions flooded my mind. If the word *race* only dates back to the 1700s, did that mean people weren't organized by skin color before that? If scientists studying genetics are saying there is "no biological basis for races," how does that affect the way we categorize people? And what does it mean if *race* is now "primarily a sociological designation"? I was so confused.

Next, I turned to the US Census Bureau for answers. After all, an official government entity responsible for collecting data about race should know whether it is a "social construct." And once again, I found that word *social*:

> The Census Bureau defines race as a person's self-identification with one or more *social* groups. An individual can report as White, Black or African American, Asian,

American Indian and Alaska Native, Native Hawaiian and Other Pacific Islander, or some other race. Survey respondents may report multiple races.[3]

Not only was race *not* a biological category, it was a matter of self-identification. Now I had even more questions. I looked up the Census Bureau's definition of *ethnicity*, thinking it would bring clarity. It didn't. It said that ethnicity determines whether a person is of Hispanic origin or not. For this reason, ethnicity is broken out in two categories, Hispanic or Latino and Not Hispanic or Latino. Hispanics may report as any race.[4]

So, according to the Census Bureau, was being Greek or Korean *not* an ethnicity? I still had so many questions.

It turns out Census Bureau definitions have changed over the last 150 years. For example, it considered Mexicans to be "white" until 1930, then removed the category of "Mexican" altogether by 1940, only to bring it back in 1970, when various versions of the term *Hispanic* were added.[5] In light of this, I had to consider the possibility that *race* didn't have as clear-cut a meaning as I thought. But a "social construct"? That was such a strange idea to me. I could see I needed to dig deeper into history.

THE DEVELOPMENT OF RACIAL HIERARCHIES

History can be boring when it's presented as just a list of dates, but it becomes illuminating when we understand it as the second half of the word: *story.* A moment in history is like the last domino in a line: It falls over because a hundred other dominos fell before it. The ideas and theories that are popular today got their start long before most of us were born. The modern concept of race is no exception.

It turns out that modern race consciousness is a relatively new phenomenon. Before the seventeenth century, when the term *race* began to emerge in general English usage, it typically referred to a group sharing the same ethnicity, language, and national origin. In other words, French, English, German, and Jewish people all would have been considered separate races under the original definition. The focus on skin color—and the movement to classify people based solely on physical features—is an unfortunate legacy of the Enlightenment.[6]

During the Enlightenment, a growing number of intellectuals became interested in scientifically categorizing living things. Immanuel Kant's 1775 essay, "On the Different Races of Man," pioneered the effort to migrate the term *race* into its modern usage. Kant divided humanity into four races: Whites, Negros, Hunnic (Mongolian or Kalmuck), and Hindu, appealing to superficial observational data to account for racial differences. For example, he argued:

> The superabundance of iron particles, which are present in all human blood, and which are precipitated…through evaporation of the acids of phosphorus (which make all Negros stink) cause the blackness that shines through the superficial skin; and the high iron content of the blood seems also necessary to avoid slackening of all parts. In short, the Negro is produced, well suited for his climate; that is, strong, fleshy, supple, but in the midst of the bountiful provision of his motherland lazy, soft and dawdling.[7]

This kind of language strikes us as offensive today, but it laid the groundwork for what eventually became racial distinctions and racism.

Shortly after Kant's essay was published, a naturalist named Georg Forster traveled around the world with his father and Captain James Cook, the British explorer, observing many different cultures. Forster's book, *A Voyage Round the World* (1777), described in detail the customs of the native people he encountered. His description of indigenous women reflected the eighteenth-century European ideal of beauty.

> Among the spectators we observed several of the prettiest women of this country; and one of them was remarkable for the whitest complexion we had ever seen in all these islands. Her colour resembled that of white wax a little sullied, without having the least appearance of sickness, which that hue commonly conveys; and her fine black eyes and hair contrasted so well with it, that she was admired by us all.[8]

Kant's and Forster's ideas paved the way for the development of modern race theory. Facial characteristics, hair texture, and skin color started to become core features of human identity, producing a domino effect in how Western societies thought about human beings and their value. But it was all based on a flawed understanding of what it means to be human. So, in the sense that the modern notion of race comes from their superficial classification and valuation of human beings, it seems accurate to say that race is a social construct.

WHY GEOGRAPHY MATTERS MORE THAN RACE

Kant hypothesized that race was essentially a biological category 75 years before the publication of Darwin's *On the Origin of Species*. He didn't have the backing of modern science for his ideas, and he didn't know anything about genetics or their influence on superficial physical traits.

Thankfully, science has caught up with the truth of Scripture. The completion of the Human Genome Project in 2003 has provided a provocative new way to investigate the issue of race. Advancements in genetics have allowed scientists to gain insight into human origins and early migration. And, in a way, that enables us to test the biblical account of shared human origins. On the surface, the physical differences between an Asian and a black African seem dramatic. But a growing body of scientific research supports the idea that humans are, in fact, one group, not many. In the 2017 article "New Gene Variants Reveal the Evolution of Human Skin Color," geneticist Sarah Tishkoff from the University of Pennsylvania explains, "Many of the gene variants that cause light skin in Europe have origins in Africa."[9]

Differences between racial groups are determined by only a tiny portion of the human genome. While physical traits such as eye shape, skin color, and hair texture do vary, the traits we share as a species are far greater than our differences. The few differences that do exist are generally the result of environments and other external factors. In short, we're all cousins.[10] This is consistent with the biblical picture of human origins (Genesis 3:20; Acts 17:26).

The best way to understand our physical diversity is by connecting it to the geographical origins of our ancestors. If we look at a map of the "old world" (prior to the massive migration into the Americas), we can see that humans with more melanin lived closer to the equator, while those with less melanin lived further from it (map p. 71).

What accounts for this? Without getting into all the details, let's assume that humans originated somewhere between modern-day Iraq (see Genesis 2:10-15) and Northeast Africa (where most scientists place the first humans). As some people migrated into northern latitudes, their pigmentation lightened due to microevolutionary changes (also known as *adaptation*) over time. People with darker skin have historically lived closer to the equator. Those people who

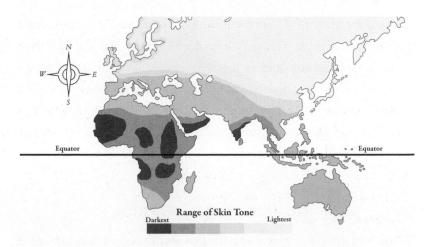

migrated farther away from the equator into Asia and Europe lightened as they adapted to cooler climates.[11]

While Kant correctly guessed that biology contributes to the physical differences between groups, he was completely wrong about the causes. The mounting evidence that humans are more alike than different ought to encourage us, as this data undermines the idea that superficial physical differences define our value. The data also relegates belief in racial "purity" and the intellectual superiority or inferiority of certain races to the category of pseudoscience.

These discoveries, however, don't totally erase differences between ethnic groups. Certain populations may be more prone to heart disease, diabetes, or neurological disorders than others. For example, populations with multigenerational exposure to malaria can be more susceptible to sickle-cell anemia, and individuals of Ashkenazi Jewish descent have an increased risk of certain genetic disorders.[12] Understanding a person's ethnic background and family history can give doctors insight into which diseases to screen for with certain patients.

As scientists continue to uncover more evidence, I believe that the case for humanity's common origin will continue to strengthen, and the idea that our physical differences ought to divide us will continue to lose ground. Rather than placing others into racial categories, each of us can enjoy gaining better knowledge of our medical history and predispositions, connecting with our heritage (matters of providence), and enjoying both the similarities and differences that are part of our common humanity.

DOES GOD SEE RACE?

While our society is obsessed with classifying people by skin color, the Bible rarely references it—and when it does, it is not a central feature of a person's identity. For example, Jeremiah 13:23 says, "Can the Ethiopian change his skin or a leopard its spots? Then also you can do good who are accustomed to do evil."

Far from using skin tone as a major category, the Bible simply mentions it in passing as a physical feature. It is recognized, not emphasized. Jeremiah could have asked, "Can the grass stop being green?" or "Can rocks stop being hard?" He was simply stating an obvious, unchanging reality to make a broader spiritual point.

But the Bible *does* have a lot to say about ancestry and regional origin. The word *ethnicity* comes from the Greek word *ethnos*, which is often translated into English as "nation." The Bible also uses *ethnos* as a way of referring to non-Jewish people groups. But one of the most common mistakes Monique and I see in discussions about race in the church is the conflation of race, ethnicity, and culture. These are not the same thing! Scripture acknowledges distinctions between nations, kinships, clans, and families. These are all biblical categories, but race is not.

The Bible affirms that humans share a universal, common origin, described in Genesis 1 and 2. This is confirmed in Genesis 9 and 10.

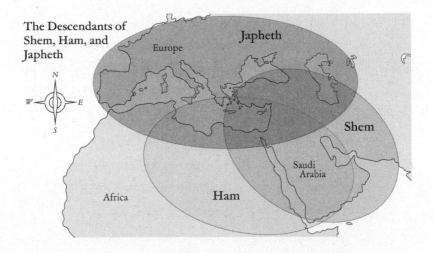

After the flood, God used Noah's sons—Shem, Ham, and Japheth—and their wives to repopulate the land (Genesis 9:19). The "Table of Nations" in Genesis 10 describes the first wave of post-flood human migration (see map above), giving us a snapshot of how Noah's descendants began to fill the earth (Genesis 9:1, 7) and spread out over the Middle East, North Africa, and even Europe. Their descendants eventually formed new nations and ethnicities.

Later, God promised Abraham that he would be the father of "many nations" and that through his descendants, all the nations would be blessed (Genesis 12:1-3; 15:1-5; 17:5-8). That blessing came through Jesus as Messiah (Matthew 1:1), and the spiritual aspect of this promise came to fruition at Pentecost, when Jews from "every nation [*ethnos*] under heaven" in Jerusalem heard the good news, each in their own language (Acts 2:5-6). Three thousand repented, believed in Christ, and were baptized that day. God's ancient promise to Abraham is still bearing fruit today as the gospel continues to spread through all nations (Matthew 28:18-20).

The book of Revelation also describes this fulfillment through the apostle John's vision of heaven:

> They sang a new song, saying, "Worthy are you to take the
> scroll and to open its seals, for you were slain, and by your
> blood you ransomed people for God from every tribe and
> language and people and nation [*ethnos*]" (Revelation 5:9).

> After this I looked, and behold, a great multitude that
> no one could number, from every nation [*ethnos*], from
> all tribes and peoples and languages, standing before the
> throne and before the Lamb, clothed in white robes, with
> palm branches in their hands (Revelation 7:9).

The "ransomed people for God" include members of every *ethnos*.
The Bible acknowledges different countries of origin, languages, geographical regions, and even regional accents (Matthew 26:73), *but
it does not divide humanity according to race as we do today*. The Bible
does not cooperate with our artificial frameworks or modern categories. If we aim to think biblically about humanity, we must ultimately
reject the modern concept of race and adopt the Bible's framework
of nations (*ethnos*), clans, regions, and languages. Adopting a biblical
framework means being careful not to read our modern notions about
race back into biblical history. This is why, for example, I believe we
need to avoid misidentifying the hostility between Samaritans and
Jews as "racial" when it appears more biblically accurate to describe
that hostility as a prejudice between two differing religious groups
who shared common ancestry. While some characterize Jesus's conversation with a Samaritan woman (John 4) as a demonstration of
racial reconciliation, the context indicates that He was simply explaining who was qualified to be part of God's New Covenant people—
that it was based on belief in Jesus as the Messiah.

Likewise, I hear people often use Miriam's conflict with Moses's
Cushite wife as an example of racial prejudice (Numbers 12:1). However,

the text gives no indication that skin color was the central concern. It's not even clear whether ethnicity played a role in the conflict at all; perhaps it was an issue of cultural or religious practice. The text simply doesn't specify. I think we would do well not to read our modern prejudices into ancient culture. Instead, we need to apply the Bible's framework over ours.

RETHINKING OUR RACIAL IDENTITIES

Many are telling us today that the most important thing about who we are is our social location. For example, I am a white, middle-class female. According to the social identity hierarchy, I am near the top. A black female with the same social status would rank lower in the hierarchy and be seen as having less earning power. Sometimes this

A few of the oppressor/oppressed groups that constitute the social binary, according to contemporary critical theory

Identity Marker	Type of Oppression	Oppressor Group	Oppressed Group
Race	Racism	Whites	People of color
Class	Classism	The rich	The poor
Biological sex	Sexism	Men	Women
Sexuality	Heterosexism	Heterosexuals	Homosexuals
Gender identity	Cisgenderism	Cisgender people	Transgender people
Physical/mental ability	Ableism	The able-bodied	People with disabilities
Age	Ageism/Adultism	Adults	The elderly/children
Religion	Religious oppression	Christians	Non-Christians
Colonial status	Colonialism	Colonizers	Indigenous people
Skin color	Colorism	Light-skinned people	Dark-skinned people

idea is called *identity politics*; academia often refers to it as *intersectionality*. People with more intersections of oppression are seen as marginalized. Those in the privileged categories are called upon to de-center their privilege and become an ally to those in the "targeted social groups."

According to this sociological framework, a person's social rank shapes their interpersonal interactions and forms not only what they believe about themselves and others, but also the language they use to describe one another. In addition, people with multiple "oppressed" identities experience oppression uniquely, and to a greater degree, in society. These ideas and ways of talking have been brought into local churches by racial reconciliation advocates, making race (a matter of providence) an essential foundation for a person's identity.

For example, Biola University Provost Matthew Hall, formerly of Southern Baptist Theological Seminary, describes his thoughts about his identity as a white man as:

> I am a racist…I am going to struggle with racism and white supremacy until the day I die and get my glorified body and a completely renewed and sanctified mind because I am immersed in a culture where I benefit from racism all the time.[13]

Hall's statements sound shocking but make sense when seen through the lens of intersectionality. This is a great example of how the sociological framework of antiracism trains us to think and talk about race as an essential part of our core identity—and how some believers adopt this language and bring it into Christian contexts. Here is where we need to make an important distinction between ourselves and most racial reconciliation advocates: If Monique and I were to sit down with most people on the other side of the conversation, we would likely strongly agree on issues related to creation identity and salvation identity.[14] Where we seem to disagree is how to weigh matters of providence.

This is because the Bible doesn't categorize or assign value to humans based on culture or physical features. Instead, it provides a framework for understanding where we came from, what it means to be human, and how we should treat one another. From a biblical standpoint, our pigmentation is not a defining feature about us. That's not to say that historical strife between ethnic groups should not be acknowledged. Those issues deserve patient understanding on all sides of the conversation. But describing the behavior, value, and demeanor of all members of a particular group simply based on skin color is to engage in the worst form of stereotyping and to miss God's unique placement of each one of us in a particular time and place.

SHOULD CHRISTIANS BE COLORBLIND?

If we had a dollar for every time a well-meaning white person (and yes, it's almost always a white person) said to us, "I don't see color," Monique could probably buy lotion for a year. (And for the record, she uses a lot of lotion!)

"Colorblindness" is the source of much misunderstanding between racial communities. Early in our friendship, Monique and I fell into this trap. She firmly believed that "colorblindness" was an insulting idea and that the term should never be used. At that time, I saw it as a noble virtue and a helpful summary of my beliefs about race. Our debates about colorblindness led to several hard conversations and eventually, an epiphany: *We were using entirely different definitions of the term!*

Monique thought I was saying, "I don't see your race." From her perspective, I was denying the physical reality that she is a five-foot-eight black woman. Consequently, I was also denying her identification (at that time) with the black struggle for liberation. Naturally she kept responding, "That's just dumb!" Meanwhile, I was using *colorblind* as shorthand for summarizing what I understood to be Dr. Martin Luther King Jr.'s vision of impartial judgment of individuals.[15]

Looking back, I now understand Monique's concern. It *is* dumb to deny physical reality. After all, Monique's physical features, including her height and skin color, are "fearfully and wonderfully made" by God (Psalm 139:13-14). She in turn has come to understand and appreciate my perspective: God calls us to judge according to people's character, not their outward appearance (1 Samuel 16:7). We both now understand how different communities use the term *colorblindness*. And we both acknowledge that this term can bring a lot of confusion into an already challenging conversation. As such, we advise Christians using the term *colorblind* to pause and define what they mean before continuing. Our goal should be clarity, not confusion.

MOVING AWAY FROM RACE

Both the biblical unity model and the racial reconciliation model agree that race is a social construct. But what separates the models is that racial reconciliation advocates also demand, at least in practice, that we make race an essential feature of a person. So while we might agree that race is not a legitimate biological category, our culture is still obsessed with seeing it as essential to a person's core identity.

These race-based messages can be very powerful, holding immense influence over our perceptions and experiences. Media, social systems, peers, and institutions regularly categorize us according to our skin color and thereby label us as "privileged" or "powerless." Constant reinforcement of these categories can keep us divided, like parallel lines that never intersect.

But even if secular society continues to promote race-based labels and ideals, Christians don't have to interact with one another that way. Instead, we can embrace a better model rooted in biblical principles. Christians are well equipped to dismantle racial categories both in principle and in practice. In principle, we reject race-based categories because they aren't found in the Bible. In practice, we can intentionally grow in our awareness of ways we may be participating in this public fiction and correct our course. One of the ways Monique and I try to do this is by using terms like *ethnicity* or *culture* whenever we can, as a replacement for the word *race*.

We need to renew our minds according to the Word of God (Romans 12:1-2) and use the principles of Scripture to deracialize our thinking and our practices, both in our churches and in our interactions with non-Christians. We can and must show the world that there is something deeper than race that unites us: our humanity. Christians lead by example. We must live in a way that demonstrates our belief in the inherent dignity and worth of every human being. We cannot offer a voice to counter the culture's conflicting messages about race if our hearts aren't first convinced that God has a better plan. Let's firmly place our confidence in that better plan.

REFLECTION QUESTIONS

1. What was your understanding of the definition of *race* before reading this chapter? How does knowing more about the history of how Western society has come to conceptualize race affect how you receive the statement that "race is a social construct"?

2. What is the difference between race, ethnicity, and culture? In what situations can being observant of someone's racial, ethnic, or cultural differences help you better connect to them? In what ways have you seen the significance of these differences be overemphasized?

3. In what ways has a modern understanding of race affected how you read the Bible?

4. How have you heard the term *colorblindness* or the expression "I don't see color" used? Do you think it's helpful or counterproductive?

5. Why is a clear and mutual understanding of a word or term's definition so essential to our conversations with both Christians and non-Christians alike? Have you seen breakdowns happen when definitions are unclear?

CHAPTER 4

WHAT IS RACISM?

Krista Bontrager

One day, Monique and I set out on a hike in a new area. The location was a little more remote than usual, the weather a little hotter. In the middle of the hike, I began experiencing heat exhaustion. As our water supply ran low, Monique quickly tried to get me to safety. More than 30 people passed us as we struggled our way out of the canyon. Many stared, but none stopped to check on us or offer help. They all kept walking.

Once we made it down the final hill to the parking area, I sat on a shaded bench while Monique went for the car. While she was gone, an older gentleman stopped to ask me if I needed help. Finally! A surge of tears and emotion spilled out. He shared his water and waited with me for Monique to return. Thankfully, he was a former track coach for a local Christian college and knew a few practical remedies for heat exhaustion. This brother in the Lord waited with me for 45 minutes. (Monique got lost!) When Monique and I finally drove away, I wondered: *Why had no one else stopped or tried to help us on the trail? Why did someone only bother to stop once I was sitting alone? Was it because Monique was black?*

Of course, I had no evidence that racism was involved, only sheer speculation. But the seed was planted in my mind. And once again, the issue turned out to be more complicated than I thought.

A SHORT HISTORY OF RACISM

In the last chapter, we surveyed how Immanuel Kant's ideas about racial hierarchies and stereotypes took hold in Western culture. Many saw black people as physically stronger, yet lazier, than white people. This idea was used to justify beating slaves to "teach" them to work. Some people thought black people smell different, so black parents made sure their children were always clean and presentable.

In 1904, the promoters of the World's Fair collected thousands of indigenous people from around the world to display as exhibits in a "human zoo." They were presented as evidence for Darwinian evolution, as less-evolved "missing links" between apes and white people. Everything from their body parts to their cultural practices were measured against the Western ideals in an attempt to popularize racial and cultural hierarchy among the general public. As many as 15 million people saw the exhibit.[1]

While such a display seems horrific to us now, those ideas were an outflow of Darwinian evolution. Charles Darwin is widely known for his book *On the Origin of Species* (1859), which became the foundation for much modern biological theory. Some would say that his second book, *The Descent of Man*, shows a darker side of Darwin's legacy. In it, he applied to race his theory of natural selection and "survival of the fittest." Darwin argued that humans evolved from an ancient, ape-like ancestor, and that the process of evolution in humans was ongoing. He classified white, Western Europeans as more evolutionarily advanced than "savages" or "the lower races,"[2] and opined that cultural progress and the development of civilization were natural outcomes of white Western European culture.

Philosophers and historians debate whether *The Descent of Man* represents Darwin's complete views on race and racism. Nevertheless, I think a case can be made that the concept of racial hierarchy is deeply embedded in that book.[3] While belief in a racial hierarchy was already gaining popularity, *The Descent of Man* played a pivotal role in lending it "scientific" and philosophical validation.

Darwin's framework inspired his successors to extend his ideas into social experiments, including eugenics. Advocates of eugenics implemented reproduction limits on non-whites, the poor, the mentally incapacitated, and the disabled. Though Darwin may or may not have supported such efforts, eugenicists clearly saw themselves as building on his ideas. "Racial hygiene" theories provided a scientific, philosophical, and moral grounding for the start of "reproductive health" organizations like Planned Parenthood, forced sterilization, and Hitler's efforts to preserve Aryan racial "purity." While Hitler represents an extreme end of the eugenics movement, similar causes were widely championed in the United States, the United Kingdom, and Western Europe as progressive and even compassionate.[4] Kant, Darwin, and others laid the groundwork for some of the darkest moments in Western history, including the enshrinement of racism.

DEFINING RACISM SOCIOLOGICALLY

Before meeting Monique, I thought racism mostly meant belonging to the KKK or mentioning that black people had dark skin. I even asked Monique once if it was racist to comment about her having darker skin than I do. She laughed so hard. "Honey, you can't miss all this melanin!" At the time, I was confused by her laughter. Now I look back and laugh at myself! My heart was in the right place, but I was clueless.

Shortly afterward, I asked Monique, "How are you defining *racism*? I think we might be using two different definitions." She answered with 100 percent confidence: "Racism is prejudice plus power." I had no idea what that even meant.

Defining racism can be difficult, but it's also vital. When we fail to define our terms, well-meaning people can talk right past each other. The definition Monique gave me then (to which she no longer holds) reflects a common sociological understanding of racism. In addition to the "prejudice plus power" definition of racism discussed earlier, I will use the glossary on the popular Racial Equity Tools website to break it down even further.[5] Six major definitions of racism come up regularly in modern conversations about race:

Individual racism includes the "beliefs, attitudes, and actions of individuals that support or perpetuate racism. Individual racism can be deliberate, or the individual may act to perpetuate or support racism without knowing that is what he or she is doing."[6] Individual racism isn't necessarily overt or aggressive toward others; it occurs in the person's mind and manifests through internal dialogue and subtle attitudes and actions. Examples may include avoiding interacting with certain ethnic groups or being especially suspicious or fearful of members of another racial group.

Interpersonal racism is what happens when individuals convert their private thoughts of prejudice into racist behaviors. Common examples could include using racial slurs and jokes in the presence of a member of the targeted ethnicity, burning crosses, advocating that one ethnic group is inherently better or smarter than another group, or refusing to let one's children have playmates of another race.[7]

Individual and interpersonal racism are the forms of racism that most people in the older generations are most familiar with. This is why baby boomers and Gen Xers frequently find accusations of racism from younger generations so puzzling.

Racial reconciliation advocates are likely referring to a different definition when they say "racism," specifically referencing institutional, structural, or systemic racism. These forms of racism are understood to include two elements: racial prejudice and institutional power. Prejudice involves bias or a preconceived belief about someone. Racial prejudice involves bias based on a person's race or ethnicity.

Institutional racism is said to involve "the ways in which institutional policies and practices create different outcomes for different racial groups. The institutional policies may never mention any racial group, but their effect is to create advantages for whites and oppression and disadvantages for people from groups classified as people of color."[8] When institutional power is used to implement or reinforce racial prejudice in institutional policies and practices, racial reconciliation advocates call this *institutional racism.*

This definition contains the assumption that white people will automatically have an advantage in getting hired or promoted if minorities aren't given special privileges. This is why some people say things like, "Colorblind hiring is racist" or "Women and minorities are encouraged to apply." When the percentage of racial minorities in a company or industry isn't proportional to the percentage of minorities in the general population, racial reconciliation advocates often believe that institutional racism is at work.

Structural racism is defined as encompassing "the entire system of White domination, diffused and infused in all aspects of society including its history, culture, politics, economics, and entire social fabric. Structural racism is more difficult to locate in a particular institution because it involves the reinforcing effects of multiple institutions and cultural norms, past and present, continually reproducing old and producing new forms of racism."[9]

A third variety of the "prejudice plus power" form of racism is **systemic racism**, which is defined as "an interlocking and reciprocal relationship between the individual, institutional and structural levels which function as a system of racism. These various levels of racism operate together in a lockstep model and function together as a whole system."[10]

In other words, systemic racism is the whole enchilada. It is all the forms of racism thrown together, interacting with each other to form an insurmountable wall for most minorities. This is the form of racism that is usually in play when you hear people say things like, "Racism is baked into every aspect of society."

According to racial reconciliation advocates, a complex set of circumstances persistently results in harmful or even traumatic outcomes for minorities. For example, if black women experience higher rates of preeclampsia during pregnancy than white women, the very existence of these disparate outcomes—no matter what factors caused them—is seen as a sign of systemic racism. The evidence for systemic racism is always found in the outcome, not always in direct cause-and-effect relationships.

One final definition of racism is believed to be the result of systemic racism.

Internalized racism is defined as "the situation that occurs in a racist system when a racial group oppressed by racism supports the supremacy and dominance of [a] group by maintaining or participating in the set of attitudes, behaviors, social structures, and ideologies that undergird the dominating group's power."[11]

Minorities who cooperate with "white structures," such as getting good grades in school, using standard English in the workplace, or complying with law enforcement, are often accused of having internalized racism, or "acting white," by their peers.

Understanding these definitions is a critical step toward having productive conversations with racial reconciliation advocates. It's also vital for testing these sociological definitions to see how they compare with Scripture.

DISTINGUISHING BETWEEN
OVERT AND COVERT RACISM

Monique enjoys retelling stories about times I've absentmindedly let doors close on her. But the reality is, I forget to hold doors open for other people—a lot. One time, we got into a tense conversation about my habit. I sat on the couch in her room while she stood in front of her mirror, giving me a TED Talk about intention versus impact. She told me that *intent* is what I want to do, but *impact* is the reality of my actions and how they land for the other person. I may not have *intended* to let the door close on her, but she *felt* slighted. That was the impact.

She kept telling me the only thing that mattered was impact. Finally, I stopped her. "I get it that intention isn't everything. But it's also not *nothing*. It's *something*. It's data."

We were both exasperated. Eventually, she conceded that I had a point…at the end of the conversation, when she tried to explain her *intention* for doing something that had frustrated *me*.

Intention and impact are key concepts in discussions about *covert* and *overt* racism. Everyday, garden-variety verbal or nonverbal snubs or lapses in manners by white people are often seen now as examples of covert racism or "microaggressions." Today, every interaction between a white person and a black person is assumed to be, by nature, a racialized situation. It's not a matter of *if* racism is involved in the situation, but *how*. Therefore, even small acts of rudeness by white people are seen as miniature acts of oppression and white supremacy.

Many employers are holding employee trainings about microaggressions in an attempt to regulate these covert racist behaviors within organizations. If an employee feels that a microaggression has occurred, it's common to label such actions as violent, racist, or even traumatic without first investigating intent. It's now no longer necessary to prove that overt racism has occurred (see the chart on page 89). When an incident occurs, the deciding factor for a guilty verdict rests almost exclusively on the recipient's subjective perception of its impact.

The problem is, so-called microaggressions may have nothing to do with racism at all. A rude coworker may be rude to everyone, regardless of race. Perhaps the perceived "aggressor" simply had a bad day, never learned common courtesy, or doesn't understand that something that is acceptable in one culture is rude in another.

Seen through the lens of microaggressions, the people passing by us on the trail that day or my door-closing habit could be labeled as "covertly racist" without any investigation into heart posture. When I let the door close on Monique, the truth is, I'm often distracted by my own thoughts. I have ideas for podcasts, things I need to tell my husband when I get home, and a miles-long to-do list zooming through my mind—and then I allow the door to close after me. I am simply a serial door nonholder. I'm working on doing better.

Sadly, the racial reconciliation and antiracism models would likely label my actions as racist despite my not having poor intentions. Because I am white, even unintentional slights toward minorities are seen as the outflow of my "whiteness" and participation in an invisible system of white supremacy. Microaggressions only go one direction: from white people toward minorities. And my intentions don't matter.

Except they do.

Monique and I believe the concept of microaggressions is unbiblical. The alleged victim often becomes an unchallenged authority, and the offending words or deeds are deemed covertly or overtly racist. It places the "victim" in the role of judge, able to discern the intentions and guilt of others without evidence. Instead, the Bible gives clear instructions that God's people should judge rightly (Deuteronomy 1:16; 16:18; John 7:24). Biblical justice requires us to judge impartially (Leviticus 19:15), investigating the evidence in a situation through multiple witnesses (Numbers 35:30; Deuteronomy 17:6; 19:15;

Overt

KKK • Lynching

Jim Crow laws • Genocide

Hate crimes • Swastikas • Racial slurs

Forced cultural assimilation • Racist jokes

Confederate flag • Mass incarceration • "All lives matter" • Police brutality • Tokenism

"Two sides to every story" • Euro-centric curriculum • White person speaks over POC

White savior complex • "You don't sound black"

Celebrating Columbus Day • White silence • "Get over slavery"

Anti-immigration policies • English-only initiatives

Expecting POC to teach white people about race

"One human race"

Not challenging race jokes

"Colorblind" society

Covert

2 Corinthians 13:1). As we weigh the evidence, Christians must also work from a posture of love, which includes rejoicing in the truth and believing the best about others (1 Corinthians 13:7). We must also keep in mind that only God can fully and accurately judge the motives of the heart (1 Corinthians 4:4-5).

Racially motivated slights can and do happen. We don't deny that. Perhaps some people selectively allow doors to slam on people of a different ethnicity or refuse to hire them because they dislike "those people." If careful investigation and verifiable data show this to be the case, that action might rightly be seen as racist and dealt with accordingly. But not every hurt feeling or bruised toe is evidence of racism. It is not the root behind every hard conversation or complicated situation involving people of different ethnicities. Christians must rely on evidence, aiming for objectivity as we investigate whether sin is being committed. If we rely on our feelings to arbitrate truth, we may be led astray (Jeremiah 17:9).

WHEN SOCIOLOGY SHAPES OUR THEOLOGY

When Christians speak of racism, we need to define the term carefully. All too often, well-meaning churches and ministries release statements condemning racism without taking this step. Whenever possible, Christians need to go the extra mile to offer a clear definition shaped primarily by Scripture, not sociology.

Many Christian leaders have adopted the sociological definition of racism as "prejudice plus power." One prominent pastor from Philadelphia, Dr. Eric Mason, has promoted aspects of this framework. In a 2021 sermon, he said:

> Racism is different than prejudice…Prejudice is a biased or preconceived opinion about someone. So prejudice is the ability to have a disposition toward someone. But racism is the ability to enact your power based on your prejudice against someone. *Anybody can be prejudiced. Only a few people can be racist.* So racism is the application of your power to enforce your prejudice on people that you want to enforce it on.[12]

In affirming the framework's second claim, he said:

> That means whites have to stop calling black people racist. You [can] call a black person prejudiced. But you can never

call a black person racist. Because the difference between me and you is [that] I can call you whatever crazy racial slur I want, I can *not* treat you a particular way, but racism is a bit different. It's me using my *structural* capacity in connection to power, to enforce my prejudice and to cut things off from you.[13]

I appreciate that Mason went on to affirm that God's power and providence can overcome racist situations, but by accepting the sociological definition of racism, he seems to be affirming the view that racism is a sin unique to white people.

We disagree.

DEFINING RACISM BIBLICALLY

Another day, another daily walk, and yet another tense discussion about race. In the middle of the conversation, a question leaped to my mind and out of my mouth. "Are you aware that there is no verse in the Bible that says, 'Thou shalt not be a racist'?"

That blew Monique's progressive social justice mind. So we began sorting through all the confusion about racism by going to the Bible first. Sifting through ideas requires an authoritative, trustworthy framework. That's exactly what God's Word gives us.

The reality that all humans are created in the image of God (Genesis 1:26-27) forms the foundation for the Christian response against racism. This aspect of our creation identity provides the ground for human dignity and value. This idea played an important role in abolishing the transatlantic slave trade.

Since the word *racism* is not in the Bible, however, we need to ask: Does Scripture address the concept? After all, the word *Trinity* isn't in the Bible either, but the key concept of God as triune is clearly present throughout. The answer is no—the modern concept of race itself is a social fiction, an idea that is foreign to Scripture. For this reason, we try to use the term *ethnic partiality* in the place of *racism* as often as possible. We think a case against ethnic partiality, prejudice, and behavior can be made through the Bible's condemnation of three distinct sins.

Engaging in favoritism or partiality. God is impartial (Ephesians 6:9). He doesn't play favorites. He doesn't love Jews more than Gentiles (Acts 10:34; Colossians 3:11), men more than women, or the rich more than the poor (Galatians 3:28). God cannot be bribed (Deuteronomy 10:17; 2 Chronicles 19:7). Regardless of our status here on earth, each of us will one day stand before God's judgment seat and give an account for all our actions, whether good or bad (2 Corinthians 5:10; Colossians 3:25). This is true equity: God judges everybody by the same standard.

He also wants His people to use His standards of justice, which is why He repeatedly forbids judges to accept bribes (Exodus 23:2-3; Leviticus 19:15) and commands His people, particularly the leaders, to judge impartially (Exodus 18:21; 1 Timothy 5:21; James 2:1, 9). We are not to judge others based on arbitrary or superficial criteria such as skin color, ethnic background, national origin, or socioeconomic status. God's heart for His people is to use an objective standard based in His character. So we are to examine each individual's character (1 Samuel 16:7; 1 Timothy 3:1-7) and establish multiple lines of evidence before reaching a judgment (Deuteronomy 19:15; Matthew 18:16; 1 Timothy 5:19). This is what it means to judge someone fairly.

To clarify, not all forms of partiality are unbiblical. I *ought* to be partial to my husband over all other men (Genesis 2:24; Matthew 19:5-6). It's not immoral to buy my child a piece of candy, even if I don't buy candy for everyone else's child. It isn't wrong to reward an honest employee with a strong work ethic and not others, or to avoid surrounding ourselves with corrupt people (Proverbs 22:24;

1 Corinthians 15:33). Protecting the vulnerable may require performing background checks on caregivers and discriminating against applicants with certain criminal histories. This is not unjust, but wise.

Harboring hatred toward a person or group. Sin always begins in the human heart, then manifests in our actions. God's standard of holy living isn't simply about curbing behaviors, but about transforming hearts. The apostle John makes this clear:

> Whoever says he is in the light and hates his brother is still in darkness...whoever hates his brother is in the darkness and walks in the darkness, and does not know where he is going, because the darkness has blinded his eyes (1 John 2:9-11).

Hating someone due to their skin color or country of origin has no place in the life of a Christian. This hatred can then be manifested through our behaviors, breaking other aspects of God's justice, such as through murder or theft.

Using dehumanizing words toward other people. Slurs and snubs must not be accepted among Christians. Verbally cursing a fellow image bearer is unjustifiable for Christians, even if our culture embraces the practice. It's true that regulating our speech is a difficult task. As James 3:5 points out, the tongue is a "small member" of the body but can spark a (figurative) forest fire. James 3:9-10 says,

> With [the tongue] we bless our Lord and Father, and with it we curse people who are made in the likeness of God. From the same mouth come blessing and cursing. My brothers, these things ought not to be so.

Racist or ethnic slurs toward other groups are displeasing to God—and so are slurs cast toward "our own." Whether it's a white person calling others "white trash" or "cracker," or African Americans calling other African Americans things like "coon" or "Uncle Tom," none of these should be accepted among Christians.

When Monique began publicly migrating away from the racial reconciliation model toward the biblical unity model, both white *and* black people began calling her horrible names. She was now seen as "outside the tribe" because her thoughts and words didn't align with the majority of African Americans. Members of her own community cast racial slurs in her direction. *Even Christians.* One phrase often used among African Americans to describe tribal "traitors" like Monique is "skin folk, but not kinfolk." In other words, "You may look like us, but you don't think like us, so you're no longer one of us."

This behavior labels certain types of people as *less valuable* than others. Sadly, every culture and subculture develops these kinds of dehumanizing words and phrases about those outside the tribe. Christians must be vigilant against thinking or verbalizing slurs. If we are to change the way we think and speak about others, we must rely on the power of the Holy Spirit to transform our hearts and tongues.

A DIFFERENT MODEL FOR CLASSIFYING ETHNIC PARTIALITY

The desire to stand against ethnic-based partiality is good. But evaluating situations according to the numerous sociologically based definitions can get confusing, not to mention that some of them aren't compatible with the Bible. Monique and I use a simple two-part framework to talk about partiality.

Individual Partiality

This form of partiality includes the attitudes and behaviors that individuals engage in toward each other. This might range from unspoken heart postures (like hatred) to race-based assumptions (biases, prejudices), verbal slurs, favoritism, or unwarranted exclusion, and even violence. *Anyone and everyone* is capable of engaging in individual partiality toward another person or group. We cannot find any biblical warrant for the belief that only white people can be racist or that black and brown people cannot participate in any form of racism. All humans are vulnerable to all sins in thought, word, and deed.

Our position is that some form of ethnic partiality is present in every culture. It just looks different depending on where you live, whether it's the remnants of the caste system in India, historical rivalries between Asian countries, or members of two different tribes in South Africa. Ethnic partiality is a result of our fallen human nature in Adam, and for that reason, it is part of the universal human condition.

Corporate Partiality

Corporate partiality is what happens when a group colludes to give an individual or group an advantage over another on the basis of ethnicity, and then enacts laws, written policies, or unwritten practices in businesses, churches, schools, or government-run institutions.

Scripture records several examples of this. Pharaoh enslaved the Israelites and commanded midwives to kill newborn Jewish boys (Exodus 1:15-22). Herod slaughtered boys under two years old in and around Bethlehem (Matthew 2:16). King Nebuchadnezzar, the governors serving under King Darius, and the Persian official Haman all targeted Jews for destruction (Daniel 3:1-30; 6:1-28; Esther 1:1–10:3). Each story demonstrates how people sometimes leverage institutional positions to target specific ethnic groups and create policies to disadvantage, dehumanize, or even kill them.

For us, the workplace is where corporate partiality often occurs. Hiring practices are particularly vulnerable to this; a credible body of research indicates that employers often engage in "name discrimination." For example, in 2021, economists at the University of California, Berkeley and the University of Chicago revealed the results of a large-scale audit.[14] They sent 83,000 fake job applications for entry-level positions to 108 companies, including many top-tier businesses. Applications with similar qualifications were submitted in pairs, one with a more white-sounding name, such as John or Kathy, and the other with a more ethnic-sounding name, like Shaniqua or DeShawn. Researchers found that candidates with black names got fewer calls for interviews than similar applications bearing white names. These findings align with many previous studies.[15]

This is an example of what Monique and I consider an arbitrary and unbiblical form of partiality. It's not based on any objective criteria, such as an applicant's skills, job experience, and references.

As Christians, we need to make a conscious effort to look beyond the superficial. Monique and I recommend that hiring managers implement practices such as blind applicant review and posting clearly written hiring qualifications. This can help overcome unwarranted bias. If workplaces continue to promote race-based labels and policies, Christians need to consider to what degree they will cooperate with them. Race-based hierarchies contradict the clear teaching of the Bible. Christians ought to be at the tip of the spear in efforts to dismantle racial hierarchies, both in principle and in practice. Ask the Holy Spirit to help you know to what degree you are to cooperate or push back in your spheres of influence, and be prepared to obey whatever He tells you to do.

FINDING FREEDOM

I don't know if racial differences influenced people to pass by me and Monique the day I got heat exhaustion in the canyon. It's possible. But other reasons are also possible. Perhaps they thought since Monique was helping me, they didn't need to. Maybe the bystander effect was at play and most people simply thought, *Someone else will stop to help.* Maybe it's because we didn't ask for help. Without evidence or conversations with the people who walked past, I can't draw any final conclusions.

The good news is that we don't have to carry the burden and hurt of believing that others' behavior, though frustrating and potentially hurtful, is necessarily driven by racism. As followers of Christ, we can rest in letting God adjudicate those matters; only He knows the answers to those questions. And that's a wonderful thing.

REFLECTION QUESTIONS

1. How do you think Christians should approach the dichotomy of intention versus impact? How can you respond when someone says they have been harmed by your behavior, even though your intentions were good?

2. Why is it essential to define racism biblically? Where and why does the idea that racism is a sin unique to white people hurt how Christians understand each other and themselves?

3. How does understanding the sociological definitions of the various forms of racism equip you to engage with others in conversations about race, racism, and biblical unity?

4. Regardless of whether it relates to race, when in your own life do you find yourself falling into the trap of assigning guilt based on intentions you've assumed? How can you put into practice the biblical command to judge rightly?

5. Consider the quote from the end of this chapter: "Christians ought to be at the tip of the spear in efforts to dismantle racial hierarchies, both in principle and in practice. Ask the Holy Spirit to help you know to what degree you are to cooperate or push back in your spheres of influence, and be prepared to obey whatever He tells you to do." Are there any situations in your own life (or even attitudes in your own heart) where you need to begin pushing back against racial hierarchies of any kind?

CHAPTER 5

HOW SHOULD WE THINK ABOUT SYSTEMIC INJUSTICE?

Monique Duson

In the Inland Empire area of Southern California, summer temperatures can easily climb over 100 degrees, but even so, it was an abnormally hot day. And it wasn't just the weather; I was boiling on the inside. My conversation with Krista on systemic injustice was making the summer heat seem fairly mild by comparison.

In those early days of our friendship, I saw race-based systemic injustice everywhere. What made our dialogue even more frustrating was that Krista and I approached conversations on it with few definitions or facts. It took Krista about ten conversations just to understand what I meant by "systemic racism."

As we walked that day, we both regurgitated information seen on social media and made assumptions about the data (and each other) based on what "made sense" to us. I assumed that systemic injustices only impacted people of color. Krista assumed that systemic racism was completely a thing of the past. She kept pointing out that segregation no longer exists and that a black man had held the highest office in our nation.

"What systems are holding you back?" she asked. There I was, frustrated at having to explain things to white people, so I shot back with this: white people hold the majority of the power in society, and most judges, politicians, police officers, lawyers, and *Fortune* 500 CEOs are white and uphold the systems and structures that support black disenfranchisement.

Bless my little social justice heart. Krista's inability and seemingly blatant refusal to understand systemic injustice angered me. And on that day, we were willing to argue until the other person came to their senses or until we reached the front door of the house, whichever came first. (It was extremely hot, after all.)

This conversation typifies the binary mindset people often fall into when discussing systemic racism. One side insists that systemic racism is purely a thing of the past. In contrast, racial reconciliation advocates usually argue that systemic racism is embedded into the fabric of our country, even today. In a 2022 article in *Relevant* magazine, Derwin Gray states, "I am concerned about the racism that is seen only as an individual sin issue but dismisses the *historic systemic racial injustice* that is baked into existing structures that have governed American society."[1]

I don't fit neatly into either of these camps. I believe systems that target particular ethnic groups can and do exist, but I don't think they look the way that racial reconciliation advocates usually describe them. I also believe that any person or group can be victimized by systems that disadvantage them.

DEFINING SYSTEMIC INJUSTICE SOCIOLOGICALLY

The conversation about systemic racism within the United States is nearly as old as the conversation on American racism itself. In 1881, only 16 years after emancipation, American abolitionist Frederick Douglass wrote:

> Slavery had the power at one time to make and unmake Presidents, to construe the law, dictate the policy, set the fashion in national manners and customs, interpret the Bible, and control the church; and, naturally enough, the old masters set themselves up as much too high as they set the manhood of the Negro too low. Out of the depths of slavery has come this prejudice and this color line... Slavery is indeed gone, but its shadow still lingers over the country and poisons more or less the moral atmosphere of all sections of the republic.[2]

Douglass captured the idea that racism was more than the personal prejudices people hold in their hearts. Racism was embedded within laws and deeply influenced many aspects of society—the moral atmosphere.

In some ways, antiracist advocates Robin DiAngelo and Özlem Sensoy echo Douglass, defining racism as "white racial and cultural prejudice and discrimination, supported by institutional power and authority, used to the advantage of whites and the disadvantage of peoples of color."[3] They argue that "racism encompasses economic, political, social, and institutional actions and beliefs that systematize and perpetuate an unequal distribution of privileges, resources, and power between Whites and people of Color."[4]

Racism is seen as malleable and pervasive, constantly shifting forms to protect the interests of white people. Christian author Jemar Tisby often puts it this way: "Racism never goes away. It just adapts."[5] Derrick Bell, the legal studies professor who pioneered much of the post-civil rights conversation about race, said that successful efforts to counter racism are merely "short-lived victories that slide into irrelevance as racial patterns adapt in ways that maintain white dominance."[6] Antiracism frameworks are simultaneously characterized by a sense of near hopelessness and an endless dedication to the struggle against systemic racism. This is why many advocates of both antiracism and racial reconciliation sometimes sound as if they believe slavery ended last year rather than 150 years ago.

According to them, dominant Eurocentric social norms always disadvantage racial minorities (except for some Asians, who are often called "white adjacent"). When Christian leaders, like Jude 3 Project founder Lisa Fields, describe racism as America's "original sin," the insinuation is often that systemic racism is a cancer endemic in American history and society, creating an insurmountable obstacle to the success of minorities—and that it will never be cured without white people recognizing historic wrongs and acknowledging current systemic injustice and white complicity.[7]

RACIAL RECONCILIATION AND SYSTEMIC RACISM IN THE CHURCH

Racial reconciliation advocates in Christian spaces often build their case for systemic racism on three key arguments: the Hellenistic widows, racial injustices in America's past, and disparities.

First, the case of the Hellenistic widows, which is found in Acts 6:1-7, recounts a dispute from very early in the church's history, when "a complaint by the Hellenists arose against the Hebrews because their widows were being neglected in the daily distribution" (v. 1).

In October 2020, the Gospel Coalition released an interview in which Reformed Theological Seminary staff member Philip Holmes was asked to give a biblical example of systemic racism.[8] Holmes went right to Acts 6:1-7 and argued that it described what was primarily an ethnic dispute.

> The text doesn't talk about how [the system against the Hellenistic widows] was happening. It could have been intentional or it could have been unintentional. The text is vague; it's just vague. It just says that there was a system that was in place. So the apostles get together and changed the system. I think this is helpful and applicable to how we think about our systems today and how we think about the sin of systemic racism or systemic injustice.[9]

While I agree with Holmes that the text leaves out a lot and that there did appear to be some kind of broad system in place to aid the early Christians in Jerusalem, we don't know the exact nature of the problem. Something was happening in the distribution of resources that resulted in the Greek-speaking Jewish widows being neglected. But what exactly was it? The text does not indicate this system was created to intentionally target the Hellenistic widows due to their ethnicity. We don't know why Luke includes the ethnic heritage of the two groups in question. I believe Holmes goes beyond the text when he says the Hebraic Jews "favored a particular group over and against the Hellenistic Jews."[10] As far as we know—and as Holmes points out—this oversight could have been unintentional. Maybe the Hellenists were overlooked because the distribution occurred at the time the widows usually did laundry. Maybe there was a language barrier. Maybe more devout Jews were opposed to the way Hellenistic Jews borrowed beliefs and practices from Greek culture during the Diaspora. We just don't know!

The text also doesn't support the frequent claim that the apostles appointed deacons in order to "change the system." Neither does it say that their goal was to knock down the whole system and rebuild it because #HellenisticLivesMatter. In fact, they may not have changed the system at all. Perhaps the deacons came and instructed the widows about the correct time and location to show up for the distribution. Maybe they firmly told the Hebraic Jews not to be jerks and to get their pride in check. We simply don't know.

Claiming that systemic racism was the critical problem here is an overreach of the text. Unlike today's culture, the Scriptures don't train us to see everything through the lens of race. The larger context indicates that Luke's main point in this passage was to record the reasons for deacons being installed. While their names were Hellenistic, it's debatable whether that was the key factor in their appointment. The text explicitly says these men were selected based on their character, which was "of good repute, full of the Spirit and of wisdom." (Acts 6:3).

Finally, we must keep in mind that this is a descriptive text. It doesn't indicate any imperative about what churches must do today. Still, racial reconciliation advocates often use Acts 6:1-7 as their key biblical support for the concept of pervasive systemic racism. A long list of injustices is usually then produced—everything from the school-to-prison pipeline (the policies and institutional practices that disenfranchise minority [especially black] and poor children, putting them on a pathway toward criminality instead of college and career), to wealth inequities, to the fact that your mother's knitting group consists mostly of white people, as evidence for systemic racism being embedded into everything, everywhere.

AMERICA'S ROUGH HISTORY WITH SYSTEMS OF RACISM

After discussing Acts 6:1-7, many racial reconciliation advocates go on to make a case for current pervasive systemic racism that stems from American history. Discussions like this can be confusing, as not everyone has the same extent of historical knowledge. Krista, for example, knew a lot more about our country's founding principles and documents while I knew more about things like Black Codes and redlining. In the beginning, neither of us really knew what the other was talking about.

When discussing systemic racism, it's important to help people have a basic understanding of at least three historical examples of systems of racism. The degree to which these examples still impact people today can be a point of respectful discussion and disagreement, but the historical facts are something all can agree on.

Jim Crow Laws

The compromise of 1877 brought an end to the era of Reconstruction in the South and ushered in the era of Jim Crow. Although slavery came to an end in 1865, Jim Crow codified a complex network of laws that relegated African Americans to perpetual second-class status, legally mandating their segregation from white spaces. The landmark Supreme Court case *Plessy v. Ferguson* (1896) made segregation legal, as long as the treatment and condition of spaces provided for black people were equal to those provided for white people. But they were almost always dirty, dilapidated, and run down—never equal to white spaces.

Black Voting Rights

Most know that the Voting Rights Act of 1965 outlawed Jim Crow–era voting discrimination against black people in many southern states. What is less well-known is that it was one of four laws passed to accomplish that goal. After the Civil War, the Fourteenth and Fifteenth Amendments to the Constitution (ratified in 1868 and 1870, respectively) granted citizenship and voting rights to black people. Sadly, with the end of Reconstruction and the installation of Jim Crow and Black Codes, voting rights for former slaves in most southern states were functionally rescinded at the local level.

Black voters faced hurdles such as literacy tests, poll taxes, the "grandfather clause"[11] (stipulating that only people whose grandfathers had voted were allowed to vote, effectively eliminating the voting rights of descendants of slaves), intimidation, and sometimes even physical punishment. The Civil Rights Act of 1964 prohibited poll taxes, and in 1965, the Voting Rights Act ended all other forms of voter discrimination, including literacy tests.

Redlining

Redlining involved a complex network of laws and practices that confined home ownership for certain groups to certain geographical areas. Since this practice often affected minority homebuyers the most, it has sometimes been called "housing segregation."

President Franklin Roosevelt's New Deal established the Home Owners' Loan Corporation (HOLC) in response to the housing crisis resulting from the Great Depression. The goal was to help create home-buying opportunities for Americans by offering financing to new buyers with longer repayment terms. This would hopefully allow Americans to gain wealth through homeownership and give jobless Americans construction work.

There was one problem: this opportunity was primarily offered to white Americans. The Federal Housing Administration (FHA) was formed and, as part of its risk-appraisal process, warned banks against lending to black people. Loans and insurance were often denied to black homebuyers and to whites wanting to purchase a home within or near a black community. According to a 2012 article published in the *American Prospect*,

> If a [black] family could afford to buy into a white
> neighborhood without government help, the FHA
> would refuse to insure future mortgages even to whites

in that neighborhood, because it was now threatened with integration.[12]

The Fair Housing Act, passed in 1968, outlawed redlining.[13] Some people argue, though, that it still occurred in some parts of the United States well into the late 1990s because of systems and biases already in place.

Those who hold that systemic racism exists today regularly use historical examples like these to demonstrate that racism has shaped our nation and continues to be an underlying operational factor in our institutions, including education, banking, and the judicial system. They believe these systems continue to disadvantage people of color because of unconscious national or personal biases. In other words, it is so deeply embedded in our systems that we assume it reflects the natural, inevitable order of things.[14]

I agree with racial reconciliation proponents that our country has a rough history with racism. I also agree that teaching this history, including the laws and practices that overtly targeted minorities and other people should be a standard part of American education. These systems were real, and thankfully, many have been dismantled. *But affirming historical realities doesn't automatically prove that the sociological definition of systemic racism is true.* We can accept that some systems were initially set up to benefit white people and unfairly work against people of color while still rejecting the faulty idea that systemic racism is just as pervasive today as it was in 1963 or 1863.

THE PROBLEM WITH DISPARITIES

The third component in the case for systemic racism is racial disparities. Racial reconciliation advocates usually shift from talking about history to pointing to current examples of gaps between white people and people of color, including the wealth gap, police targeting minorities, higher rates of pregnancy-related deaths in the black community, and higher incarceration rates for black men. These disparate impacts are usually interpreted as the result of systemic racism and an enduring consequence of slavery, Jim Crow, and redlining.

Systemic racism, they say, prevents minorities from having full and equal access to education, jobs, and housing. These barriers will be removed and a better future for minorities made possible through dismantling "the system" and constructing a new system committed to racial or restorative justice. Aspects of this new system include recruiting and hiring more "diverse" candidates, restructuring our education system, intentionally promoting people of color to higher levels of power, funding black-owned and -led businesses, and redistributing wealth. The goal is *equitable* outcomes. But this emphasis often leaves out certain data sets and ignores the role of personal choices and preferences—which is why black people may be overrepresented in the NBA and underrepresented in, say, accounting or classical music. Economist Thomas Sowell makes this point when he writes,

> The conversation around disparities and equal outcomes is often misleading and is actually only seeking to alleviate racism and disparate outcomes for some. Black players overwhelmingly represent the NBA—more than 70 percent are black, while whites make up less than 20 percent. Should we now protest and restructure the NBA to make it more equitable toward whites wanting to join the sport? In 2000, the U.S. Commission on Civil Rights released data advising 44.6 percent of black applicants were turned down for the most desirable mortgages while only 22.3 percent of whites were turned down. This report fueled a lot of conversation and anger regarding systemically racist housing policies. However, no one mentioned that,

for those same mortgages, whites had been turned down 22.3 percent of the time compared to Asian Americans and Native Hawaiians, who were only turned down 12.4 percent of the time. Is this also evidence of systemic racism? Information left out of data reporting and automatically seeing disparate outcomes involving black or brown people as definitively racist misleads people and moves us away from potentially needed conversations to arguing about things that may not actually be issues at all.[15]

While I once held this view, I am no longer convinced that systemic racism is a helpful lens through which to identify the problem or the solution. Conversations with experts in a variety of fields, combined with my own research of peer-reviewed literature, biblical texts, and experience working in social service, has given me a different perspective. While demonstrating the negative impact of past racial injustice on black Americans is easy, proving that most negative disparities in the black community today are due to systemic racism is, in my view, impossible. Too many human variables are involved in creating disparate outcomes.

WHAT ABOUT UNCONSCIOUS BIAS?

Disparate racial outcomes are often said to be caused by unconscious or implicit bias, defined as "the negative associations that people unknowingly hold" which are "expressed automatically, without conscious awareness."[16] The concept of the unconscious is rooted in psychology, beginning with Sigmund Freud. Carl Jung later built on Freud's work and argued that "the personal unconscious"—the unknown thoughts or repressed or forgotten memories or experiences of the individual—can materialize by influencing behaviors.[17] Those ideas have recently been applied to the subject of race and serve as a foundation for unconscious bias trainings used in many secular companies and Christian ministries today.

The stated intention of this kind of training is to help employees discover the biases they are assumed to have. They typically address racial biases held by the dominant group—usually white people. As one popular training document explains,

> Most people in the dominant group are not consciously oppressive. They have internalized the negative messages about other groups, and consider their attitudes toward the other group quite normal.[18]

I can see some value in exploring beliefs people may have about members of another ethnic group, such as "all Asians are smart" or "many black men are thugs." Helping people inspect why they may interact with others in a particular way and appreciate the unique gifts and life experiences of a different group can be valuable for better collaboration. But the problem is, many of these trainings engage in the very stereotyping they claim to decry, focusing almost exclusively on highlighting white biases against minorities and dismissing the possibility that white people might sometimes be the target of race-based *dis*advantages. This view dismisses any racism aimed toward the dominant group and, oddly, sees any disagreement with this framework as proof that unconscious racial bias is at work. Dissenters and questioners are often labeled as covertly racist or as a minority with internalized racism.

IT'S NOT JUST ABOUT
THE SYSTEMS YOU SEE

When I began questioning my views on racial reconciliation, I had a pivotal conversation with Dr. Pat Sawyer, a professor at the University of North Carolina Greensboro, about systemic racism. Pat was the first person to explain the difference between *de jure* and *de facto* systems to me, a distinction that provided a more nuanced way of thinking about systems of injustice. And he helped me step outside the false dichotomy of believing either that there is no such thing as systemic racism or that systemic racism is embedded into everything.

De jure (Latin for "from the law") systemic racism is racism codified into law and backed by the state or federal government and enforced "by law and public policy."[19] Progress in fighting *de jure* racism can be seen through the ratification of the US Constitution's Thirteenth and Fourteenth Amendments, the Fair Housing Act, and the Civil Rights Act. These laws overturned previous laws and provided a legal foundation for equal treatment for members of all races.

De facto (from the Latin for "from the fact") systemic racism refers to the factual observation, or reality, that some form of injustice is happening. *De facto* systems can show up even where there are no laws in place. For example, while segregation has been outlawed in the United States, the management of a "whites-only" golf club could initiate an unwritten practice preventing new members of certain groups from joining. While there is no *de jure* policy at the golf club, there is a very real *de facto* system in place limiting opportunities for some groups.

I have found the distinction between *de facto* and *de jure* systems to be a very useful way to help me detect whether ethnic partiality is in play in a particular situation. Krista and I also use an additional criterion, whereby we differentiate between "macro-" and "microsystems" of injustice. A macrosystem involves a complex web of laws and policies that reach across multiple institutions and has large-scale impact. Redlining could be considered an unjust macrosystem, as it reached across multiple government agencies and had widespread impact. Microsystems are smaller-scale situations, such as a company's methods of screening job applicants or the unequal treatment of customers at a particular restaurant.

Sinful systems can be built at macro or micro levels because sinners exist. Wherever there are sinners—of any ethnicity—sinful systems are possible. But the fact that some sinful systems exist doesn't automatically prove that racial injustice is "baked into society at every level." We doubt that systemic racism exists on the scale its advocates assert. When evaluating a potential case of systemic racism, it's helpful to start with some probing questions, such as:

- Are we discussing a past or present example of a racist system?

- Are we discussing a *de facto* or *de jure* form of a racist system?

- Are we discussing a macrosystem or a microsystem?

- What data show a direct cause-and-effect relationship?

One time, we did a staff training for a major international Christian ministry. Roughly 80 percent of its thousands of employees in that region were black, but all members of the top management team (about 70 people) were white. We immediately began asking questions and gathering data.

The ministry's statement of faith disavowed racism, so we gave them the benefit of the doubt and assumed there wasn't a *de jure* policy that only white people could hold senior leadership positions. Therefore, we began probing to see if a *de facto* system might be in place. When we asked about criteria or methods used to promote qualified candidates, the top leader said they screened candidates by "asking the Holy Spirit." I responded, "So, in a hundred years, the Holy Spirit has never prompted you to promote a black person?" We weren't able to explore this issue in detail with that ministry, but from our perspective, an unwritten cultural practice—a *de facto* policy—seemed to be at work. As a regional-level problem, we would consider this a microsystem of *de facto* racism. If the practice extended across the ministry's global offices, that would constitute a macrosystem of racial partiality.

INTERRUPTING SYSTEMS THROUGH PERSONAL RESPONSIBILITY

Too often when I speak to young black teens, they tell me "the system" is holding them back. My first thought is, *White people are not your biggest problem.* I believe the real challenge for all children born into poverty and violence—regardless of ethnicity—is to get a different vision of what life can be. When all you see around you are broken families, drug addiction, and gangs, it's not easy to imagine there are alternatives.

Claims of systemic racism too often push the roles of individual responsibility out of the conversation. These are topics that need more discussion, and that's why my friend Kevin Briggins and I host *Off Code*, a podcast addressing issues within the black community. We both grew up in predominantly black neighborhoods and have seen the moral failings of individuals blamed on entire systems of whiteness. This negates the autonomy of the individual and makes systems the primary wrongdoer, not the person actually harming others by their negative actions.

Biblically, we know that God will hold each individual accountable for his or her actions (Matthew 12:36; Hebrews 4:13). And, as Kevin likes to say, "If all our problems are the result of white people, then we are at the mercy of white people to fix them. We have no agency and are completely reliant upon those we claim are our oppressors to deliver us."

While I was growing up in poverty-stricken areas, I saw horrible violence, as did most of my friends. But systemic racism was not our biggest problem. Most of my childhood friends are now accomplished professionals with solid educations and well-paying jobs. Most of us made it to a better life through a combination of personal choices, making the most of the opportunities that came our way, and accepting help from youth leaders, teachers, and mentors. That's not to say it was always easy or that some of us didn't make wrong turns along the way. But what we did *not* do was sit around and wait for white people to create a new magical system to rescue us.

Personal responsibility applies both to those who witness injustice and those who believe they may be victims of injustice. If a Christian sees systemic or individual forms of (biblically defined) racial injustice in motion—regardless of which ethnic group is being advantaged or disadvantaged—that individual has a responsibility to say or do something (within biblical bounds) to interrupt the flow of the system. They can draw attention to biblically defined injustices, work to prevent them, and find ways to improve systems to eliminate ethnic partiality.

Blaming your problems on poorly supported claims of systemic racism results in a sense of helplessness, fueling frustration and even anger about seemingly insurmountable barriers. But it doesn't need to be this way. Minorities don't need to feel pinned down by the weight of history or as if they're unable to seize the opportunities available to them, and members of dominant ethnic groups don't need to feel pressured to swoop in to save the day or constantly prove themselves to be good "allies." Instead, both can take responsibility to make wise personal choices and stand up against any biblically defined injustice, racial or otherwise, that they encounter. And that's empowering.

REFLECTION QUESTIONS

1. What aspects of history discussed in this chapter surprised or challenged you? Are there any ways in which this chapter has changed how you view the concept of systemic racism?

2. Consider the Jim Crow Laws, the Black Voting Rights Act of 1965, and the practice of redlining. How do these support the history and evidence of systems of racism? How can people misuse these truths to overemphasize the current scale and impact of systemic racism?

3. In light of this chapter, how would you define systemic injustice? Consider the statement, "Affirming historical realities doesn't automatically prove the sociological definition of racism is true." Do you agree or disagree with this? Why?

4. As a Christian, what role do the concepts of agency and personal responsibility play in your faith? Where in the Bible do you see these concepts examined?

5. How does personal responsibility apply both to those who witness injustice and those who are victims of it?

CHAPTER 6

SHOULD CHRISTIANS WORK TOWARD RACIAL RECONCILIATION?

Krista Bontrager

One day, while we were out on our routine walk around the neighborhood, Monique kept emphasizing the need to get everyone to "the table." Once again, I was lost. In a moment of exasperation I asked, "Where is this table, exactly? And how do I get there?"

Monique seemed to know everything about the "right" way to talk about race and racism, and I was…well, the white person who just didn't get it. I felt dumb and discouraged. Getting to "the table" of racial reconciliation felt like an elusive, unachievable goal. But because of our close friendship, I genuinely wanted to understand Monique's perspective and concerns. And if I needed to correct something about myself, my behavior, or my thought patterns to approach this table, I was committed to doing that.

So I began doing my own research. I listened to more than two hundred hours of podcasts. I read books and articles by thought leaders such as Latasha Morrison, Jemar Tisby, and Eric Mason. These seemed to be the "approved" Christian voices who knew the way to that elusive table. Monique and I frequently talked through what I was reading and processed the content together while we walked.

My journey to the table turned out to be a long and winding road. Spoiler alert: I did eventually claim my seat. And I'm going to tell you how to do the same.

But first, let me tell you how not to.

DO THE WORK, LEARN THE RULES

I eventually learned that "getting everyone to the table" is a favorite theme of racial reconciliation advocates. Sometimes the table is literal; people are encouraged to invite members of other ethnicities to their dinner table for conversation and to build relationships. Often, the table is figurative, and "getting to it" refers to the proper way to participate in discussions about race.

The demand usually rests most heavily on white Christians. For example, in June 2020, Pastor Al Tate from Fellowship Church in Monrovia, California, delivered a sermon called "The Family Table" about doing the work of racial reconciliation. While sitting at a literal table, he exhorted congregants not just to sit around but to "stay at the table," even when the conversation gets hard. He lamented the challenges of staying at the table, saying, "When we start having real conversations about real pain and real things that hurt us…and it gets in the sight line of our idolatry, how quickly we get up from the family table and take our ball and go home."[1] While Tate didn't explicitly identify white people as those who are most apt to "leave the table" and "take their ball and go home," he did describe his response to a white commenter who "didn't want to talk about race and oppression" on his livestream earlier in the morning:

I don't want to talk about race and oppression, either. I'd love to change the subject. But in order for me to change the subject, I'd have to change my skin color. I'm inviting you to a table to listen to something I actually live with. So while I'm sorry that it's hard for you to listen, imagine how hard it might be for me to live it.[2]

In most cases, those seen as holding up "everyone" from getting to the table are white people. It's frequently assumed that minorities—at least those who are aware of injustices—are already there, ready to engage in conversation. The near-universal assumption is that it's the white people who aren't ready. This is why you will frequently see messaging geared toward helping white people take steps toward the table. Prominent campus ministry, InterVarsity, has an entire article to this effect on their Multiethnic Ministries site titled, "4 Steps White People Can Take towards Racial Reconciliation."[3] The assumption seems to be that people of color are already engaged.

CAN "DOING THE WORK" BRING TRUE UNITY?

Many racial reconciliation advocates use language that invites people to become "allies" and "do the work" to build bridges across ethnic and cultural divides. This is a worthy goal. And Monique and I agree with Pastor Tate when he admonished his congregation that the table Christians sit around must be a "bloodstained table," referring to the blood of Christ.[4] Truly, the gospel is what unites us as Christians, and it ought to motivate us to stay committed to one another, even through hard conversations.

But we usually disagree with racial reconciliation advocates on how the goal is defined and how they want to reach it. Latasha Morrison calls Christians to do the work by being "bridge builders." Her organization, Be the Bridge, and book of the same name, have shaped how many in the church believe reconciliation should be accomplished. She describes the connection between reconciliation and restoration this way:

> Reconciliation is the restoration of a broken relationship between two people or groups of people. Reconciliation happens when an agreement is reached about a former dispute; then restitution is made, forgiveness is granted, and true communion begins to develop between the formerly divided people or groups.[5]

Morrison and other racial reconciliation advocates assert that this restoration process requires everyone to acknowledge the historic injustices of the past (something we generally agree with) and implement sweeping policy changes throughout our institutions, including government, businesses, churches, and schools (something we may not agree with, depending on biblical warrant, available data, and the solution proposed). Because racial reconciliation advocates generally accept the sociological definition of systemic racism and insist that it is pervasive in society, the way problems are identified and solutions are proposed can be deeply flawed.

In the secular context, the "work" of antiracism may include things like having organizations establish offices of Diversity, Equity, and Inclusion and hiring full-time DEI officers; the government reclassifying certain crimes as misdemeanors rather than felonies; and foregoing school suspensions or homework deadlines for minority students.

The racial reconciliation model within the church calls for deliberate efforts to facilitate healing, build true diversity, and establish trust between the races. But advocates say the "bridge" between racial groups cannot be built until each member of the dominant group (generally, white people) acknowledges his or her complicity in unjust systems. They also must humble themselves and listen to the stories of pain and trauma from those who have experienced forms of systemic racism. The hope is that this process will result in empathy and advocacy for racial minorities.

In Morrison's online resource "16 Bridge-Building Tips for White People," she provides a list of principles for conduct while learning about racial reconciliation. These "bridge-building" tips are typical of racial reconciliation literature. For example:

> **#2 Don't take up too much (metaphorical) space in the conversation.** Yes, this is hard for verbal processors. We know you have important things to say, but White people's ideas and stories are prioritized everywhere else. Take this opportunity to sit quietly and elevate the voices of [people of color].

> **#9: Don't demand proof of a POC's [person of color's] lived experience or try to counter their narrative with the experience of another person of color.** The experiences and opinions of POC are as diverse as its people. We can believe their stories. But keep in mind: just because one person of color doesn't feel oppressed, that doesn't mean systemic, institutional racism is not real.

> **#11: Do not chastise POC (or dismiss their message) because they express their grief, fear, or anger in ways you deem "inappropriate."** Understand that historically, we White people have silenced voices of dissent and lament with our cultural idol of "niceness." Provide space for POC to wail, cuss, or even yell at you. Jesus didn't hold back

when he saw hypocrisy and oppression; POC shouldn't have to, either.[6]

When I first read Morrison's rules, I didn't understand why racial reconciliation required me to provide space for an angry black person to cuss or yell at me. Why were unbiblical ways of speaking to each other allowed for some but not for all? I asked Monique, but she just directed me to the first rule on Morrison's list:

> **#1: Don't expect POC to be your only source of education about race.** Black, Indigenous, and people of color get exhausted explaining the same ideas over and over again, every time a white person "joins the conversation." Read a book instead. Watch a documentary. Google terms and ideas. If you must hit up your friend of color for insight, at least buy them dinner, and really listen to what they have to say.[7]

"I'm not Google," Monique said one day during our walk. "I can't do your research for you."

It seemed that "racial reconciliation" simply meant assigning me a list of rules to follow solely based on my skin color. The only requirement for Monique or any other black person was to correct me when I didn't obey the rules.

How could this framework possibly lead to genuine unity?

ASSUMPTIONS OF RACIAL RECONCILIATION

A critical assumption Morrison and other racial reconciliation advocates make is that the path to reconciliation is determined by people of color who think a certain way. The methods, outcomes, and assumptions of this model cannot be questioned by anyone, *but especially not by a white person.* In fact, asking questions is often viewed as confirmation of either "internalized racism" (if you're a person of color) or "white fragility" (if you're not). Those who are still asking questions aren't ready for a seat at the table.

Many racial reconciliation advocates operate under the assumption that participating in these efforts is simply what faithful disciples of Jesus ought to do. Coming to the table requires participating in a particular way: agreeing that the problem is systemic racism, and that the solution is for white people to acknowledge and repent of their participation in systemic racism.

Moreover, they also must participate in *ongoing acts* of racial reconciliation to remain in good standing, such as advocating for the redistribution of wealth and power. In their minds, these are necessary steps to loving one's neighbor as Christ commanded.

While I desperately wanted to be on board with Monique's vision for racial reconciliation and set right anything that might be amiss in how I saw the world and treated others, I couldn't accept an entire framework and its moral code without examining its soundness.

If the foundation was firm, I knew I could trust the framework— but I still had questions. What is the *biblical* foundation for all of this? Where did these voices get their authority? Because clearly, getting everyone to the table for the conversation isn't enough. The real goal isn't conversation; it's getting everyone to adopt the same vision for restoration as the only legitimate solution.

A BETTER PATH TO RACIAL UNITY

One of the most important underlying assumptions embedded in the racial reconciliation framework is that races need to be reconciled. This sounds good, but is it biblical?

Christians who advocate for racial reconciliation consistently refer to 2 Corinthians 5:18 (God "gave us the ministry of reconciliation") and Ephesians 2:14 (Christ "has broken down...the dividing wall of hostility") as key texts for demonstrating that the Bible calls us to work toward this goal. The problem is that they seem to neglect the full context.

In his book *Woke Church*, Dr. Eric Mason outlines a common two-step process connecting 2 Corinthians 5:18 to racial reconciliation efforts.

> This is the glorious gospel! We have been reconciled to God
> by the death of Jesus Christ. We rejoice in that truth. But
> in the gospel, man is not just reconciled to God by faith.
> Man is also reconciled to man by faith. (See 2 Corinthians
> 5:18.) God has given to us the ministry of reconciliation.
> He doesn't give us the luxury of refusing to be reconciled.
> If God could pursue reconciliation with us—in spite of
> all of our sins, our rebellion, our issues—we should be
> rushing toward one another to reconcile.[8]

The near context, as well as the theme of the book overall, makes it clear what kind of reconciliation Mason has in mind: *racial* reconciliation. His two steps to racial reconciliation are as follows: (1) Sinners who believe in the work of Jesus on the cross are reconciled to a holy God, and (2) because of this act, Christians should pursue reconciliation with one another.

Another well-known pastor, Dr. Tony Evans, uses the same two-step framework in his book *Oneness Embraced* when he writes,

> When we get radical believers who take seriously the
> apostles and the prophets and the teachings of Jesus Christ

the way we were called and created to do, we will reconcile people vertically to God as we reconcile people horizontally to each other in Christ's name.[9]

This "cross-shaped" framework is generally summarized this way: We reconcile with God and then reconcile with each other.

Overall, we respect Dr. Evans's ministry and believe he is a biblically-sound teacher, but we disagree with his interpretation of this particular Scripture passage. While it's true that the gospel does have implications for how Christians treat one another, and God has clearly given His people the "ministry of reconciliation," there's more to the story. The key question that must be answered is: Who is being reconciled to whom?

Paul answers this clearly in 2 Corinthians 5:10-15: Someday we will all stand before God for judgment and will receive what is due to us. Because we know God's justice is coming, Christians ought to be motivated by a holy fear and love for others to call non-Christians to become reconciled to God through Jesus so that their sins will not be counted against them.

The "reconciliation" Paul refers to is very specific: reconciliation between sinners and a holy God. He makes this clear in verses 16 to 21.

> From now on, therefore, we regard no one according to the flesh. Even though we once regarded Christ according to the flesh, we regard him thus no longer. Therefore, if anyone is in Christ, he is a new creation. The old has passed away; behold, the new has come. All this is from God, who through Christ reconciled us to himself and gave us the ministry of reconciliation; that is, in Christ God was reconciling the world to himself, not counting their trespasses against them, and entrusting to us the message

of reconciliation. Therefore, we are ambassadors for Christ, God making his appeal through us. We implore you on behalf of Christ, be reconciled to God. For our sake he made him to be sin who knew no sin, so that in him we might become the righteousness of God.

Paul says that God gave Christians the "ministry of reconciliation" and the "message of reconciliation," both of which involve calling non-Christians to "be reconciled to God." In contrast to Mason and Evans, we believe Paul's two-step framework for Christians looks like this: (1) Remember that someday everyone will stand before God to be judged, and (2) tell those who are far from God how to be reconciled to Him.

Paul's intended message in this passage is not a push to take specific steps to reconcile races, ethnicities, rich and poor, or any other division between Christians. It is, however, about explaining our salvation identity in Christ and our commissioning to share the gospel.

In verses 16 and 17, Paul describes an amazing effect that reconciliation between sinners and a holy God will have: the creation of a new people. Those who have been reconciled to God are part of a new subset of human beings: those who are "in Christ." Members of this group are different from the rest. They are a "new creation."

And that's the real game changer. Let's take a deeper look at Ephesians 2:11-22.

Paul's thoughts in this book are divided into two major sections: the theological basis for Christian unity, which he explains in the first three chapters, and instructions for how to live out unity in Christ, which he covers in the remaining three chapters.

In chapters 1 to 3, Paul unfolds the "mystery" the Father "purposed in Christ, to be put into effect when the times reach their fulfillment—to bring unity to all things in heaven and on earth under

Christ" (Ephesians 1:9-10 NIV). According to Paul, the Father's plan is to bring all things under Jesus's authority and rule (1 Corinthians 15:20-28), including calling out a new people from among the nations who are unified under Jesus (Ephesians 2:14-19). Paul explains that God "predestined us for adoption" to become His children and coheirs with Christ (Ephesians 1:5).

This is a key point. The New Testament abounds with family language. God is our Father (Acts 1:4; Romans 1:7; Ephesians 6:23). Christians are spiritual brothers and sisters (Mark 3:33-35; Ephesians 6:21), parents (Titus 1:4), and members of the Father's house (Ephesians 2:19). Our identity as a supernatural family isn't a small, tangential side issue. Family is a core component to how we are to relate to one another as Christians.

In Ephesians 2:12, Paul calls his audience to "remember that you were at that time separated from Christ, alienated from the commonwealth of Israel and strangers to the covenants of promise, having no hope and without God in the world." Most Christians in Ephesus were Gentiles—non-Jews who were outside of God's covenant with Israel. In verses 2 and 3, Paul describes them as following the course of this world, following the prince of the power of the air, living in the passions of their flesh, carrying out the desires of the body and the mind, and by nature children of wrath. Not exactly a flattering description! Yet, this is God's description of our position prior to being "in Christ." But Paul doesn't leave it there.

> But now in Christ Jesus you who once were far off have been brought near by the blood of Christ. For he himself is our peace, who has made us both one and has broken down in his flesh the dividing wall of hostility by abolishing the law of commandments expressed in ordinances, that he might create in himself one new man in place of the two,

so making peace, and might reconcile us both to God in
one body through the cross, thereby killing the hostility.
And he came and preached peace to you who were far off
and peace to those who were near. For through him we
both have access in one Spirit to the Father (Ephesians
2:13-18).

The word translated "but" in English should catch our attention.
Paul is creating a contrast with his previous description. The unflat-
tering spiritual profile *was* true of the Ephesian Christians, but now
something entirely different *is* true of them. For those who are in
Christ, a major shift has taken place. The Father, Son, and Holy
Spirit have made a way for those who were once far from the Father
to become His children. Even Gentiles. Paul, then, is talking about
something that has already been done, not something we are required
to work toward.

BREAKING DOWN HOSTILITY

When Paul talks about making "us both one," he is not primarily
describing tensions between ethnic groups. And the "dividing wall
of hostility" is not between blacks and whites, but between unre-
deemed people and a holy God. God simultaneously breaks down
this "wall of hostility" and creates a new people. The mystery of the
gospel is that God invites members of every nation to trust in Jesus
as their Messiah and come into a covenant relationship with Him.
Because of Jesus, former ethnic or social divisions (matters of providence) between Jews and Gentiles have been dissolved. Under the
Old Covenant, the division was between those inside God's covenant
with Israel (Jews and Jewish proselytes) and those outside the covenant (Gentiles). Under the New Covenant in Christ, the primary

differentiation between people, in God's eyes, is between those who are "in Christ" and those who are "in Adam." Anyone, Jew or Gentile, who does not trust in Christ remains "in Adam" and in their sin. Anyone, Jew or Gentile, who places faith in Jesus is redeemed and therefore "in Christ." Those in Christ are no longer divided—regardless of our ethnic backgrounds. We are fellow heirs, fellow citizens in God's kingdom, and something new altogether: God's family. As Paul puts it:

> Through him we both have access in one Spirit to the Father. So then you are no longer strangers and aliens, but you are fellow citizens with the saints and members of the household of God, built on the foundation of the apostles and prophets, Christ Jesus himself being the cornerstone, in whom the whole structure, being joined together, grows into a holy temple in the Lord. In him you also are being built together into a dwelling place for God by the Spirit (Ephesians 2:18-22).

WE ARE FAMILY

The main point of 2 Corinthians 5:17-18 and Ephesians 2:11-22 is for Christians to understand their mission and identity. More specifically, their salvation identity. The ministry of reconciliation that Christians are called to entails proclaiming the good news that the Messiah has come, and inviting people from every nation to come be a part of His new community. Thus, if Christians are going to live out our salvation identity and abandon a "worldly point of view" toward each other, we need to reconsider how we think and speak about ourselves (2 Corinthians 5:16 NIV). Whatever cultural or social identity we may have as a matter of God's providence, including our ethnicity, socioeconomic status, or sex, must take a back seat to our salvation identity. This is why Monique stopped referring to herself as a "black woman who's a Christian" and now simply says "I'm a Christian woman who happens to be black." *Her primary identity is Christian.*

WE'RE ALREADY AT THE TABLE

The more Monique and I studied the details of Scripture, the more we came to believe: *God doesn't actually have a plan for* racial *reconciliation.* There are no biblical mandates to gather at a sociological table or to reach equity goals. There is no separate process for groups to get reconciled to one another after they are reconciled to God. Instead, Scripture tells us that because we are reconciled to the Father through the Son, we are to participate with one another as members of God's family.

When sinful people reconcile with a holy God, a whole new reality begins for them. Christ has already accomplished what humans cannot on their own: making cultural enemies into family. Imagine a family going to court to adopt a child. Once the decision is made and the judge's gavel falls, a new reality is created. The child is now a full member of that family. From our heavenly Father's point of view, the gavel has fallen: Christians *are* family. And we cannot do anything to make us *more* family. For the Christian, unity is the reality that we live from, not a goal to be achieved one day. *This is biblical unity.*

The biblical unity model is countercultural, but being countercultural is a normal part of the Christian life. This framework lifts the burdens culture wants to place on all of us. Instead, we are free to view one another as our heavenly Father sees us: as children of God and coheirs with Christ. God's children, from all over the world, *already* have a seat at the table—but it's not the table of racial reconciliation.

If you are putting your full confidence and trust in Jesus as the Messiah, then your seat is secured at the marriage supper of the Lamb (Revelation 19:7-10). Because of this, we can be generous with forgiveness, repentance, kindness, joy, patience, humility, and gentleness as we exhort one another to be faithful to Christ and His Word.

Monique and I found freedom in knowing there is no further work that either of us must do to become more reconciled to each other. *All the work to make us family has already been done by Jesus!* While we still have room to grow in understanding one another's cultures, we no longer have to carry the weight of seeing one another through a racial lens before anything else. We can leave the world's false code of holiness. We are free to see one another through God's eyes. And you are too.

REFLECTION QUESTIONS

1. In the context of conversations about racial reconciliation, how is the concept of "the table" defined? As Christians seeking unity, how can we flip this concept and use it as an opportunity for compassion and fellowship?

2. Compare and contrast the gospel of "doing the work" that is preached in racial reconciliation to the Bible's gospel of unity through Christ.

3. What is the biblical definition of reconciliation? What does this look like and mean for you in practice? How does this influence how you approach interracial unity?

4. What does it mean to put your "salvation identity" first? Right now, are there any other identities you are prioritizing?

5. Consider the statement, "Christians are family. And we cannot do anything to make us more family. For the Christian, unity is the reality that we live from, not a goal to be achieved one day." Do you agree or disagree with this? Why?

CHAPTER 7

HOW DO WE WALK IN UNITY?

Monique Duson

●●

When I transitioned off the mission field in June 2018, I firmly believed that black people, as a group, continued to be victimized by systemic racism in a society that was committed to the empowerment of white people. And I had very firm ideas about how this problem was to be fixed. Most of my ideas were rooted in the concepts of racial reconciliation. Without this, even though we might politely call ourselves "brothers and sisters in Christ," there could be no true unity.

Imagine hearing me explain all the pieces of racial reconciliation during a 45-minute walk. Now imagine listening to me talk about it nearly every day for more than a year. That was Krista's journey with me. I'm grateful she chose to keep walking with me, both literally and figuratively. She tried her best to understand my perspective, even on days when my words probably would have made it more comfortable for her to walk alone.

A BROKEN FRAMEWORK FOR UNITY

While I agreed that Krista and I were both Christians, I hadn't thought deeply about what that meant for our sisterhood in the Lord. I didn't have a strong theology concerning the body of Christ, the church as our spiritual family, or what Paul meant in Ephesians 1 to 3 when he talked about unity in Christ. Most of my beliefs about how to "do unity" with white people had been shaped by the racial reconciliation model. Krista and I both wanted to reach racial unity, but we were taking completely different paths to get there.

We understood *unity*, and how to achieve it, differently. In my view, unity began with the acknowledgment of the horrific atrocities people of color had experienced. My beliefs at that time sounded a lot like sociologist Neil Smelser's when he said, "By 'unity' I mean commitment to a common culture and mission, a sense of solidarity, lack of conflict, and a generally positive attitude toward others in one's social category."[1] Unity could never be achieved without white people standing in solidarity with people of color, working to end racism, classism, and sexism, and all the other "isms." Only then would there be peace between the races.

In my mind, the spiritual unity Krista and I shared in Christ didn't mean that any sort of racial unity had been achieved. We (okay, mostly she) still needed to "do the work" to reach that kind of unity. For me, racial unity was a destination, not a starting point. Racial reconciliation was a pathway to unity and justice. I often quoted Micah 6:8 as my biblical support for this: "He has told you, O man, what is good; and what does the LORD require of you but to do justice, and to love kindness, and to walk humbly with your God?"

What I didn't see was that this elusive "table of reconciliation" still had people sitting in groups, sectioned off by their skin color. The table was segregated. Do you sit in the seat of those who listen, or of those who share their pain? In my mind, if white people were serious about "doing justice" on behalf of black people, they needed to understand their participation in systemic racism and recognize how society privileges all white people. Racism was embedded in every fiber of the American fabric. White people enslaved black people. White people hung black people. White people created the Black Codes and Jim Crow laws. I believed the lie that says, "If you're white, you're racist." While it certainly was my role as a black woman to keep calling everyone to the table, I believed it also was the role of every Christian, regardless of ethnicity.

Well-known thinkers like Cornel West, Beverly Daniel Tatum, Langston Hughes, and James Baldwin shaped my perspective. Contemporary voices, including Robin DiAngelo, Ibram X. Kendi, and Jemar Tisby have since built on their work. Now their voices are mainstream, shaping discussions about race and racism at local churches, knitting groups, adoption agencies, school boards, and even the family dinner table. Maybe even *your* family dinner table. Racial reconciliation says that ethnic minorities participate from the seat of the oppressed. Our role is to speak up, to speak truth to power, to protest injustice. As long as we are doing these things, we can say whatever we want, however we want, whenever we want, to whomever we want, no matter how racist or destructive those words might be. After all, we can't actually *be* racist because we don't have institutional power. We are the decision makers, determining who can fight with us in this struggle against racism, judging who is worthy to sit at the table.

Dr. James Cone, as we mentioned earlier, has become an extremely influential voice in the discussion about race and racism in Christian circles. Simply put, his theological framework stands at the intersection of Marxism, the black consciousness movement, and Christian theology. Cone's first book was published in 1969, and his ideas are being taught in a growing number of evangelical seminaries and universities today. Whenever you hear someone say they are interpreting the Bible through a "black lens" or the "lens of the oppressed," they have likely been influenced by black liberation theology, even if they have never heard of it. In many seminaries today, it is the ideas of James Cone, not the words of Scripture, that are shaping Christian thought on race and racism. When I first encountered Cone's works, I was hungry for thoughts on Christianity by someone who looked like me. Books written by black theologians weren't part of my classes at Biola, and at first, I didn't even know they existed. Cone appealed to a black woman longing for representation in Christian thought.

Now, after reconsidering his beliefs about white people, many of whom are my brothers and sisters in Christ, I am deeply disturbed by Cone's worldview and reinterpretation of the gospel. In *God of the Oppressed*, he writes,

> When whites undergo the true experience of conversion wherein they die to whiteness and are reborn anew in order to struggle against white oppression and for the liberation of the oppressed, there is a place for them in the black struggle of freedom. Here reconciliation becomes God's gift of blackness through the oppressed of the land. But it must be made absolutely clear that it is the black community that decides both the authenticity of white conversion and also the part these converts will play in the black struggle for freedom. The converts can have nothing to say about the validity of their conversion experience or what is best for the community or their place in it, except as permitted by the oppressed community itself.[2]

Cone's altered definition of "conversion" devalues my white brothers and sisters and clearly contradicts Scripture. Additionally, his cynicism about white people's redeemability and their role in racial reconciliation is demeaning. He continues:

White converts, if there are any to be found, must be made to realize that they are like babies who have barely learned to walk and talk...They must be told when to speak and what to say, otherwise they will be excluded from our struggle.[3]

To top it off, Cone sets an impossible goal, saying:

[Un]less whites can get every single black person to agree that reconciliation is realized, there is no place whatsoever for white rhetoric about the reconciling love of blacks and whites...Just because we work with them and sometimes worship alongside them should be no reason to claim that they are truly Christians and thus part of our struggle.[4]

Cone apparently never visited my house! We can't even get all the Dusons to agree on the rules of Uno, but he says all black people would have to completely agree when reconciliation has been realized. How would we ever accomplish *that*? His vision for racial reconciliation is elusive and burdensome. Can this really be the path to unity? Is this how Christ meant for His followers to treat one another?

As I reconsidered Cone's framework, I began to see it wasn't based on Christ's model of serving others, but on subjugation to an ideology I was beginning to doubt.

CRACKS IN THE FRAMEWORK

As I dug deeper, I discovered that none of the proponents for racial reconciliation I encountered seemed to have any agreement on how to achieve unity. And without agreement, racial reconciliation falls stagnant. While I could still sympathize with some aspects of that model, I began to doubt it could ever deliver on its promises for racial unity.

In the 17 years between the time I first heard of racial reconciliation to my first conversation with Krista, I didn't see great strides made toward that goal. Instead, I saw black anger, the repeated lambasting of whites as racist, and calls for more and more to be done about white racism within the church. In June 2020, Chick-fil-A owner Dan Cathy publicly shined the shoes of rap artist Lecrae, encouraging whites to show a "sense of shame, a sense of humility, and a sense of embarrassment" over slavery. As Cathy mentioned, "There is a time when people need to take personal action [against racism]." Lecrae responded, "And some stock in Chick-fil-A."[5] The video came under a lot of scrutiny. There is a very real sentiment that the rules of racial reconciliation, what must be done and what must be given, are in influx. What is not up for question is the idea that white people must pay something. There is still little agreement on what "racial reconciliation" means or how we will know when we've achieved it.

I am not denying that racism still exists. I am saying that the goal of bringing everyone to the table has left a lot of empty seats.

Through my conversations with Krista and time spent reading my Bible, the Lord began showing me the cracks in my beliefs about race. Specifically, He orchestrated two events that shattered my framework once and for all.

The first was an incident involving an intern I supervised as a program manager at a multisite food pantry. My intern was a young white woman from the local Christian college who came in to work a couple times a week. One day, in tears, this young woman told me her black classmates were telling white students they weren't allowed to speak in class. The same students also silenced some teachers and called for the university president to resign—simply, it seemed, because these people were white and in places of power. I found myself reminding her of her creation identity, that she was fearfully and wonderfully made with dignity and value. We formulated a game plan to help her navigate the rest of the semester, which included informing her parents of what was taking place on campus. (Parents, don't pay for your children to be bullied and demeaned!) I later confirmed her story after talking with several administrators. Shocked and saddened, I told Krista's daughter—who had become like a little sister to me—"You'd better not ever let someone talk to you like that!" After all, that's what my mother had told me: "Kiki, don't you ever let people talk crazy to you and disrespect you!" I didn't want Krista's daughter or my intern to let anyone disrespect them. Both of them had already internalized the culture's message that their voices were "less-than" because they had less melanin. And I didn't want them to carry that weight around anymore.

The second event happened shortly afterward, when I attended a black graduation at a major university in Southern California held at an African Methodist Episcopal (AME) church across the street from the school. At first, I enjoyed connecting with old friends and listening to culturally familiar music. Fred Hammond and Micah Stampley weren't in the usual music rotation at Krista's house! But as the graduation program began, something strange happened: Administrators began to pour out symbolic libations to the ancestors. Faculty members gave speeches from the pulpit demeaning white people. They called for a violent overtaking of "white" institutions "by any means necessary."

My friendship with Krista, and the ways the Lord was changing my heart, made what had formerly been tolerable now intolerable. I went home and cried. The calls to commit violence against white people didn't exclude people I cared about. The ideology doesn't let up on you because you marry into a minority ethnic group or adopt black kids. Under the framework, as long as ethnic disparities exist and you bear white skin, you are an obstacle to be overcome.

CHRISTIAN UNITY AS A REALITY

One night before bed I asked Krista if we could talk. By now I could see discrepancies with racial reconciliation. But I was concerned that if I let go of that framework, there would be no framework to fight racism or address the systems and structures where racism was deeply embedded. I thought that without racial reconciliation Christians could never get to unity. In contrast to racial reconciliation advocates, Krista argued that "man's laws tell us that the path to unity is to fix systems and structures. The problem is that man's laws cannot fix the most fundamental cause of racism: the human heart. Only God can do that." Krista's answer to racism was the gospel, but I had doubts about this.

For Krista, unity was built atop the truth of our identity in Christ. She firmly believed that any discussion about racial division had to begin with preaching the gospel. Jesus is the foundation. Because of Him, Christians ought to treat each other as God's moral laws require. But I kept wondering, *Is the gospel enough?* In early 2020, I read John 17. I mean, I *really* read it. I recommend you do too. God's plan for unity is centered on Christ. Jesus prayed that we, future believers, would be united with a unity as deep as what He shares with the Father. Oneness. In verses 20 to 23, Jesus prayed,

> I do not ask for these only, but also for those who will believe in me through their word, that they may all be one, just as you, Father, are in me, and I in you, that they also may be in us, so that the world may believe that you have sent me. *The glory that you have given me I have given to them, that they may be one even as we are one*, I in them and you in me, that they may become perfectly one, *so that the world may know that you sent me and loved them even as you loved me.*

This is not a unity that can be achieved by human effort, but instead flows out of the very nature of God. Jesus laid out a profound vision for spiritual intimacy. Just as the Father and the Son are one, so also are those who believe in Jesus as their Lord and Savior. All this is facilitated by the work of the Holy Spirit. He is "the glory" that the Son has given us (John 16:14-15).

Then I read that powerful last line in John 17:23, "so that the world may know that you sent me and loved them even as you loved me." Our unity has a very specific purpose: we are to be united *so the world may know that the Father sent the Son!*

When I read this, the conviction and joy of that revelation went straight to my heart. The blood-bought unity I had with random strangers in Christ was real. It wasn't a reality to be worked toward, but a reality to be celebrated and enjoyed now!

True Christians—those whose hearts have been transformed by the gospel and are indwelt by the Holy Spirit—are reconciled to God. As a consequence, they are members of a new family, the church. This is a work done exclusively by God—not a result of our own effort. No additional work of "racial reconciliation" can make us more God's children, more His people, or more brothers and sisters.

So, family, every time the devil tries to plant doubt in your mind about the reality of our unity, renew your mind with the truth of Ephesians 1 through 3 and John 17. We are already reconciled through Christ.

LIVING BY THE FATHER'S HOUSEHOLD RULES

One of the most common concerns that racial reconciliation advocates have about the biblical unity model is that they feel it places too much emphasis on the gospel. While they would agree with us that the gospel is the foundation for salvation, they are concerned that the conversation will never get around to justice. This concern often stems from a perception that white evangelicals were largely silent during the civil rights era. There is a widespread belief that white evangelicals simply don't care about racial justice and would turn a blind eye to it, even now.

I share some of these concerns too, but the framework of Matthew 28:19-20 has helped to reorder my thinking. As the gospel goes out, and people begin to share the same spiritual DNA by coming into God's family, we must also be taught to "obey" (NIV) or "to observe all that [Jesus] commanded."

Twenty-first-century American Christians don't often talk about things like "obeying commands." But humble obedience to Jesus's commands is an expression of our love for Him. Jesus says, "If you love me, you will keep my commandments" (John 14:15). A few verses later, He says, "Whoever has my commandments and keeps them, he it is who loves me. And he who loves me will be loved by my Father, and I will love him and manifest myself to him" (v. 21).

The foundation of the Christian life—the bedrock of our unity— is our faith in Jesus as our Savior. When we give our lives to Him, we want to live for Him each day. Because we love Him, we want to obey His commands. Jesus explained God's two greatest commandments in Matthew 22:37-40:

> You shall love the Lord your God with all your heart and with all your soul and with all your mind. This is the great and first commandment. And a second is like it: You shall love your neighbor as yourself. On these two commandments depend all the Law and the Prophets.

In other words, all the specific commands in the Bible fall under two broad categories: loving God and loving your neighbor. Loving

God provides the foundation for us to love our neighbors. The Holy Spirit changes our hearts so obeying God is what we want to do, not what we are forced to do. By entering into a deep personal relationship with our Creator, we can then cooperate with the Holy Spirit so His love flows to others through us. In this way, Jesus changes the world, one heart at a time.

The reality of our unity in Christ doesn't mean everyone in the family gets along all the time. Just like children in any family, Christians sometimes squabble, disagree, and even fight. God places parents in the home to provide ground rules for how the family will treat one another. Without healthy house rules, disrespect, dysfunction, and even abuse can become normalized. Similarly, our heavenly Father has set "house rules" for His family.

Thankfully, He is patient with us. We are His works in progress (Ephesians 2:10). Even while the Holy Spirit lives in us, every Christian still struggles with sin. Sanctification is the ongoing process of God working in us to help us grow and mature as His children. Sanctification is a process, not a straight line to glory. Sometimes it entails very real growing pains as we struggle against sin. As we cooperate with the Holy Spirit and put to death our old, sinful ways, we slowly conform to the image of Christ (Romans 8:1-39; Galatians 5:16-25).

Jesus's 12 apostles demonstrated God's model for unity. Jesus selected cultural enemies and made them the foundation of the church. He recruited fishermen, a zealot, a tax collector, and even a thief, and used them as the pillars of a world-changing movement. It wasn't easy, but because of Jesus, they grew and changed over time. Jesus does the same today. He makes cultural enemies into family now, just as He did then.

As Krista explained previously, the first half of Ephesians lays the foundation for unity, while the second half provides the Father's house rules within the family. Once Jesus has secured our unity, we must "maintain the unity" (Ephesians 4:3). The Father's household rules teach us how to walk in unity and live with one another as His children.

In Ephesians 4:1, Paul begins to explain how former cultural enemies can walk in the unity Jesus secured for us with His blood: "I therefore, a prisoner for the Lord, urge you to walk in a manner worthy of the calling to which you have been called." This command is the responsibility of *every* believer, not just some. Paul gave this command to the rich and the poor, the Jew and the Gentile, the spiritually mature and the spiritually immature.

Paul continues in verses 2 and 3 with some "how-tos" for living in this way. He tells us to treat each other "with all humility," and gentleness, with patience, "bearing with one another in love." He instructs us to be "eager to maintain the unity of the Spirit in the bond of peace." Paul's instructions here aren't new. He just restates or fills in the details of things God had already taught His people for thousands of years (see Proverbs 11:2 and 15:32, for example).

Paul's commands were as radically countercultural then as they are now. First-century Gentiles saw humility as negative, the attitude that slaves should hold due to their lowly position. But for God's people, humility is required by our Father and is one way we imitate Christ. Humility centers our focus on God, not on our ethnicity, accomplishments, socioeconomic status, or who or what offends us. Humility is the core of unity. Its opposite, pride, is often at the core of disunity.

Paul also admonishes the Ephesians to bear with one another in love. The original idea of "bear with" can be translated as "put up with." Let's be real, folks: We're not going to like everything that everyone in the family does, but that doesn't give us the right to disown them. Galatians 6:2 tells us to "bear one another's burdens, and so fulfill the law of Christ." Today we have a skewed definition of patience and love. We often participate with others only until we become uncomfortable, frustrated, or angry—then we walk away.

Patience is part of God's character. In Exodus 34:6, He reveals Himself as "the LORD, the LORD, the compassionate and gracious God, slow to anger, abounding in love and faithfulness." God's character is the true definition of patience, an attribute His people are called to emulate.

Believers must *choose* to be longsuffering, to endure difficulties, and to keep pursuing relationships. Stay in the game; don't be quick to become angry or frustrated. Why? Because we belong to each other. Because of Christ, we choose each other. This means getting serious about our theology, our obedience, and sacrificial love for each other. This was the heart posture that Krista displayed, which eventually led to me walking away from the racial reconciliation model.

A HOPE AND A FUTURE AS FAMILY

Our unity as Christians is based on who God is.

> There is one body and one Spirit—just as you were called
> to the one hope that belongs to your call—one Lord, one
> faith, one baptism, one God and Father of all, who is over
> all and through all and in all (Ephesians 4:4-6).

As believers, we share in the same salvation and baptism, we hold to the same faith and hope, and we were called by the same Spirit. If we, as believers, have the same gospel and the same Lord, is it unrealistic to think we can also be one in Christ?

The culture believes so. The gospel *couldn't* be enough—not without laying heavier burdens on some Christians than others. But Paul highlights the stark contrast between God's household and the world:

two different systems resulting in two different patterns of living. He says those who hold to the world's way of thinking are futile and "darkened" in their minds, separated from the life of God, mired in ignorance because of their hardened hearts (Ephesians 4:17-18). They have lost all sensitivity, indulge in every kind of impurity, and are full of greed (v. 19).

> That, however, is *not the way of life you learned* when you heard about Christ and were taught in him in accordance with the truth that is in Jesus. You were taught, with regard to your former way of life, to put off your old self, which is being corrupted by its deceitful desires; to be made new in the attitude of your minds; and to put on the new self, created to be like God in true righteousness and holiness (Ephesians 4:20-24 NIV).

Preserving our unity requires intentional obedience to the law of Christ. Paul calls this putting on the new self (v. 24). If a Christian's habitual behavior looks just like a non-Christian's, something has gone dreadfully wrong. Christians must not lie to each other (Ephesians 5:25). We must not steal, but instead work so that we can share with those in need (4:28). We must not hold on to unresolved anger and bitterness (4:26-27). Holding hatred in our hearts is as serious to God as murder (Matthew 5:21-22). Holding on to anger, or any habitual unrepentant sin, can become an opening for the devil to come in and distort our thinking.

Instead of living by the ways of the world, "Be kind and compassionate to one another, forgiving each other, just as in Christ God forgave you" (Ephesians 4:32 NIV). Many Christians talk about "loving your neighbor." But not everyone agrees on what kindness and compassion actually look like. This is why we need the Father's household rules. The Scriptures teach us how to express our love for God and our neighbor in concrete, real-world ways.

It's important to remember that keeping God's law doesn't get us into His family; it teaches us *how* to live *within* God's family. Learning to live by these house rules is the obligation of *every* Christian, no matter our skin color, because we are His, and we are family.

HARD CONVERSATIONS WITH FAMILY

Part of being in a family means having hard conversations. Our unity in Christ doesn't mean we won't have times of disagreement. But how we show up to these conversations is important.

Forgiveness is a central theme of the Christian faith. It is a topic that's largely missing from the race conversation overall, but especially within the church. Scripture presents a clear picture of forgiveness.

Forgiveness is the true scandal of the gospel. God forgives our massive, unpayable debt. Because of this, God sets a standard for how His followers are to forgive others of their debts, which are minuscule in comparison (Matthew 18:23-35; 6:12, 14-15). Our faith tells us we are to forgive those who have wronged us, regardless of the offense. The sin of racism is not excluded. Forgiveness isn't contingent upon the perpetrators' recognition of their crimes. To withhold forgiveness is to condemn ourselves (Matthew 6:14-15).

Biblical forgiveness means turning over whatever legal "right" of anger and bitterness we may think we have toward another person—or group of people—to Jesus and trusting Him to deal with it perfectly, according to His standards of justice, either in this life or at the final judgment, *even if the other person never repents*. In doing this, we are signing away our rights to resentment. What no true Christian can do is remain in a posture of perpetual offense with an individual, or a group of people, regardless of whether they directly or indirectly committed an offense. In fact, God exhorted the Israelites to be generous in their dealings with the Egyptians, despite the enslavement of their fathers (Deuteronomy 23:7). The children were not to hold a grudge against their parents' owners.

And even if a fellow Christian does sin against us directly, we still have an obligation to be generous in our forgiveness (Luke 17:3-4), to the point of even erring on the side of being disadvantaged in a dispute (1 Corinthians 6:1-7). Again, this is the scandal of the cross. In Scripture, forgiveness occurs between individuals. When one individual is sinned against by another, forgiveness is the biblically correct response. There is no scriptural precedent for personal forgiveness against an entire nation of people. In Scripture, when someone is harboring resentment against a people group (Jonah resented the Ninevites, Paul resented Christians), it appears that the Lord deals with the attitude of that individual's heart, which leads to repentance.

If you find yourself harboring resentment against an entire group of people (or against one person), repent. Ask the Holy Spirit to reveal what is hindering you from walking in biblical unity with your brothers and sisters in Christ. Is it bitterness or hatred? Is it entitlement, believing that a debt is owed to you, even though no sin has been committed directly against you? If you have offended someone, repent. If you are holding something against someone, go to that person and have a conversation. If you are holding resentment, anger, or bitterness in your heart, repent. It is more important for believers to walk in unity, according to the mandates of Scripture, than it is for us to hold on to our "right" to be right.

May we continually walk in the ways that Scripture declares are good and just, laying down our lives for the sake of the gospel and each other.

REFLECTION QUESTIONS

1. Reading this chapter, what changes did you feel convicted to make regarding your own approach to Christian family?

2. What connotations—whether positive or negative—do you bring to the word *family*? How can understanding believers as a family help Christians move forward in peace with one another?

3. Is there "disrespect, disfunction, and even abuse" that has been normalized in your experience of Christian family? What hard conversations might you need to have to promote peace and gentleness within this space?

4. How can humility help you navigate the conflicts surrounding race you encounter in today's culture? How have you seen pridefulness on both sides of the issue lead to further disparity?

5. Why can repentance and forgiveness be such a challenge even among believers? Is there anyone in your life right now whom you need to forgive? Is there anyone to whom you need to repent?

CHAPTER 8

SHOULD WE REPENT FOR THE SINS OF OUR ANCESTORS?

Krista Bontrager

⬤

Monique and I try to avoid getting into any arguments while doing livestreamed events, but one time, it almost happened.

In the early days of our *All The Things* podcast, we strategically avoided discussing several topics in public as we dialogued behind the scenes, trying to reach agreement first. We had private discussions with experts, read books, and discussed how we thought Scripture spoke to those issues.

Reparations was one of those topics. While there are many proposed forms (student loan forgiveness, tax breaks, cash payments), reparations generally involve some form of national payment to the African descendants of slaves in order to close the black-white racial wealth divide.

Two years into our friendship, I was still 100 percent *against* any form of reparations. Meanwhile, Monique had shifted from 100 percent for reparations to a more nuanced, "I'm not sure." Then we had that fateful livestream in the summer of 2020. We were receiving tons of messages a day from people asking questions about race and racism. We were pumping out podcasts and articles as fast as we could, trying to answer them all. Many people asked about reparations, so finally I brought it up on one of our livestreams by asking a guest for his opinion about whether the descendants of slaves were owed reparations. He could see a particular case for it. A few sentences into his answer, I felt myself shut down. I don't remember what happened after that. I just wanted the livestream to be over. After we signed off, I came undone, resulting in possibly the worst argument we have ever had. It lasted several days.

Eventually it occurred to me that I had a lot of emotions about a subject that I hadn't really researched. I had to lay down my pride and start a very long (and ongoing) journey of researching the issue. To this day, Monique and I both remain hesitant to address it publicly, largely because the issue is so polarizing. Advocates on both sides have strong feelings and tend to shout down the other.

Reparations is a complex issue. But we feel that we also need to have more solidly biblical conversations beyond what is currently happening. To simplify the discussion, we will focus on two critical questions:

1. Should the descendants of African slaves receive reparations?

2. Do white people need to repent for the sins of their ancestors?

We don't claim to have figured out every aspect of this thorny issue. But we can share some thoughts we've developed so far.

SHOULD AFRICAN DESCENDANTS OF SLAVERY RECEIVE REPARATIONS?

When Monique advocated for reparations, she pointed out to me that there is a precedent for a state apologizing for, and even paying for, its evil actions toward its own citizens. After World War II, Germany paid hundreds of millions of dollars to Israel, as well as individual Holocaust survivors. Japan paid reparations to South Korea for atrocities committed before and during World War II. In 1990, the US government sent a check for $20,000 to each internment camp survivor with an apology letter to 80,000 Japanese Americans for placing them in internment camps.[1]

But not all national reparations efforts have turned out well. Congress established the Indian Claims Commission in 1946 to hear the grievances of Native Americans over violated land treaties. Sadly, it didn't result in much justice and was disbanded in 1978. Congress also awarded more than a billion dollars for over a hundred years to Native Americans, but governmental corruption was so severe that it's hard to tell whether most Native Americans have benefited much. Despite Japan's reparations, South Korea is still struggling to resolve resentment over forced labor, colonization, rape, and other abuses Japanese soldiers committed during the first half of the twentieth century.[2]

Modern reparations advocates seek a process that somewhat echoes the biblical model of repentance and restitution. One of them, Duke University Professor William "Sandy" Darity, says reparations involve three goals: perpetrators acknowledging their involvement in a grievous injustice; restitution to individuals or communities for the effects of the injustices; and some form of closure signifying that the debt has been paid.[3]

A growing number of evangelicals are pushing for reparations as a component of racial reconciliation. In 2019, Thabiti Anyabwile published an article on the Gospel Coalition website titled, "Reparations Are Biblical," arguing reparations through the principle of restitution.[4] Duke Kwon and Greg Thompson released a full-length case in their book *Reparations: A Christian Call for Repentance and Repair* (2021).

Eric Mason has also advocated for reparations and even offered a list of things due to African descendants of slaves, including 200 years of free tuition at historically black colleges and universities, canceling every black person's student loan debt, repaying descendants of slaves who paid off their student loans, and free mental health services.[5]

Racial reconciliation advocates build their case for national reparations on the biblical concept of restitution. The Christian version of the case for reparations generally unfolds along these lines:

1. The Bible—Old and New Testament—teaches that restitution is the proper remedy for theft or loss.

2. Slavery was a form of theft, namely stealing of life and wages.

3. The US government passed laws that prevented former slaves from building wealth through homeownership.

Therefore, the descendants of slaves are owed reparations from the government in order to bridge the wealth gap created between blacks and whites.

While there are many other side features to the discussion, this is the general case. So, I'll try to work my way through these issues.

What Is Biblical Restitution?

When my daughters were very young, I often warned them to be careful not to scratch other vehicles with our car's door when they got out. One day, my young daughter accidentally scratched the car next to us. I made her write a short note of apology, including our phone number, to leave on the owner's windshield. "Why should I have to write a note?!" she yelled. "It was only an accident!"

My husband and I explained that though it was an accident, she was still responsible. Now, an eight-year-old obviously can't afford to pay for bodywork. We'd have to help her. But you can bet she'd be working weekends cleaning trash cans and windows at Grandma's house for a while so she could learn responsibility. In a similar way, God wants His people to take responsibility for injury, even when it's accidental.

The principle of restitution—compensating an injured party—is a deeply biblical idea. Racial reconciliation advocates are right to point this out. The Mosaic law provides several examples of this in action (Exodus 21–22). For example, if a man is injured in a fight, the one who injured him should compensate him for the time he has to miss work in order to heal (21:18-19). If a man steals his neighbor's livestock, he must pay the original owner double their value (22:4). Even if someone's property is destroyed by accident, compensation is due (21:28-36; 22:6). Restitution may call for the replacement of an item or for monetary compensation.

The New Testament affirms the principle of restitution, making it part of Jesus's commands for us today. Jesus's encounter with the tax collector, Zacchaeus, in Luke 19:1-10 showcases this. Tax collectors in the first century were employed by the Roman government and often collected taxes from their neighbors. They were commonly allowed to over-tax people and keep the difference. It's quite likely that Zacchaeus was a Jew. If that's the case, he would have been seen as a traitor, since he lined his pockets by stealing from not only his neighbors but his religious "brothers." When Zacchaeus encountered Jesus, he responded by promising to pay back those he had defrauded four times the amount he stole. Why? *Because he knew God's law.* Exodus 22:7 requires a thief to pay back double what he has stolen. Zacchaeus's willingness to repay double what was required of him shows his heart truly changed.

The scriptural pattern for restitution contains at least two components: First, the individual offender had to acknowledge a wrong had been committed, intentionally or unintentionally. Second, the injured party had to be paid back directly by the person who injured him. This practice relied directly on righteous individuals choosing to obey God, not on a massive, government-mandated wealth redistribution program. Forgiving debts in this way was a tangible expression of how God wanted the ancient Israelites to love their neighbors.

The best time to pay restitution to former slaves was just after the Civil War. Ideally, by biblical standards, this would have been done by slave owners repenting of their sins and obeying the transcultural principle behind Deuteronomy 15:12-15: When a servant had completed his service after seven years, he was not to be turned away empty-handed but instead supplied with basic necessities to start a new life. Slaveholders in nineteenth-century America could have provided compensation in the form of money, land, and livestock. In other words, slaveholders themselves should have provided their former slaves with an opportunity to support themselves and make a new start with their families.

The biblical standard calls for both material compensation *and* heart change (Deuteronomy 10:12, 16; Jeremiah 4:4; Colossians 2:11). It requires love and a desire to right a wrong. Sadly, many Christian slave owners didn't obey this principle or come to repentance after the Civil War.

Biblical Restitution and National Reparations Are Not the Same

The biblical principles of restitution raise some challenges for modern reparations efforts because they shift the focus from individual responsibility (the biblical pattern) to national responsibility. All the people involved in antebellum chattel slavery are now dead, so there is no way to follow the biblical pattern of restitution. Scripture provides no direct command or precedent for either individuals—or governments—to pay restitution to *descendants* of the injured five or six generations later. In fact, God makes it quite clear that individuals ought to only be judged for their own sins. Ezekiel 18 contains an extended discussion on this issue. If a man lives according to God's righteous standards, he shall live (vv. 5-9). But if that same man's son is violent, then he will be accountable for his actions (vv. 10-13). But then, let's say his son—the third generation—lives righteously, then he is not held responsible for his father's sins (vv. 14-18). God anticipates the objection: Why shouldn't the son be punished for the sins of the father? God's answer: "The son shall not suffer for the iniquity of the father, nor the father suffer for the iniquity of the son. The righteousness of the righteous shall be upon himself, and the wickedness of the wicked shall be upon himself" (v. 20). The Bible knows nothing of someone taking the great-great-grandchildren to court to get a judgment for sins of their ancestor.

This brings us to another challenge: there is no biblical precedent for national restitution. Using the Zacchaeus story to support a national reparations effort is a category error. Zacchaeus, not Rome, directly paid back the people he wronged. It is not an example of a government restitution program. It's an example of an individual following the biblical principle of the wrongdoer paying back the wronged. The closest we get is the description in the early chapters of Exodus where God moves in the hearts of the Egyptians to give the Israelites gold, jewelry, and the like. But this was a result of *God* stirring in the hearts of individuals (Exodus 3:21-22; 11:3; 12:35), not a national-level tax or the result of government coercion.

In January 1865, Union Army General William Sherman issued Field Order No. 15, which called for the settlement of black families on four hundred thousand acres of confiscated Confederate land. Each family would receive up to 40 acres to farm, a promise famously referred to as "forty acres and a mule." A few Republicans in the US Congress had been pushing for land redistribution. Sherman and

US Secretary of War Edwin M. Stanton met with key black leaders, many of whom were ministers, to discuss what should be done for the recently emancipated slaves. Lincoln approved Field Order No. 15 in January 1865, but President Andrew Johnson reversed it later that year after Lincoln's assassination. Most of the land was returned to its original owners, and many former slaves found themselves without homes or means of providing for their families. For the descendants of slaves, Field Order No. 15 represents a broken promise.

Even if Field Order No. 15 had gone through, I'm not convinced that it would have been following the biblical principles of restitution, largely because it didn't follow the biblical requirements of individual repair resulting from a repentant heart. I see Field Order No. 15 as an attempt to take the Judeo-Christian principle of restitution and try to scale it up to the national level, where the State would stand in for the individual wrongdoers. I am not persuaded there is a biblical warrant for this maneuver.

What Should We Do Now?

Reparations advocates often remind us of the reality that our government has yet to officially even acknowledge their participation in slavery, even though they have apologized for other atrocities. Their standard of justice includes the government repaying the descendants of slavery for labor theft, multigenerational trauma, as well as compensation for lost opportunities to build wealth through homeownership. Even though our country teeters on the brink of financial disaster caused by massive national debt and corrupt monetary policies, reparations advocates often point out that this same government almost overnight had trillions to disperse in stimulus checks during the pandemic and billions to send to other countries for frequently nebulous reasons. I can appreciate why so many descendants of slaves are upset.

Monique and I believe that some form of reparations will eventually be enacted. Our home state of California is already putting infrastructure in place to facilitate this type of program. The most likely outcome will be a massive tax-funded, government-mandated wealth redistribution program. We are also skeptical of the government's ability to put together a reparations program that won't replace one injustice with another. This is why we don't believe Christians should advocate for these kinds of reparations efforts, since they go far beyond what the Bible commands or allows. In addition, we agree with Bob Woodson, founder of the Woodson Center, that reparations will not solve the deeper social problems in the black community, such as high abortion rates, out-of-wedlock births, lack of two-parent families, high school drop-out rates, and poverty. These kinds of social problems are best solved within the framework of the Judeo-Christian worldview, which historically has played a large role in the black culture.

DO WHITE PEOPLE NEED TO REPENT FOR THE SINS OF OUR ANCESTORS?

Most of our early conversations about reparations left me feeling confused or sad. I was often upset by Monique's assertion that I was obligated to repent for the sin of slavery simply because I was white. In my mind, slavery had nothing to do with me. I have never owned slaves; none of my ancestors owned slaves; they hadn't even emigrated from Holland before slavery was abolished in the United States! So why should I be required to repent for the sins of a particular group simply because we shared a distant European heritage?

In Monique's mind, if the United States was truly sorry for slavery, then it would, *at minimum*, establish a national holiday commemorating the collective wrongs of our country toward the descendants of slaves. For instance, after World War II, Germany set aside an annual day to commemorate the Holocaust. This tradition helped ensure that the tragedy and the nation's wrong would not fade from its collective memory.

Christian racial reconciliation advocates generally make some combination of three arguments to advance their case for corporate guilt and repentance.

The first argument marshals several biblical passages to establish a precedent for corporate repentance over sin committed by previous generations—sometimes referred to as *identificational repentance*—including Exodus 20:5-6 and 34:6-7, Numbers 14:18-20, Ezra 9:6-15, Nehemiah 1:4-7, and Daniel 9:1-19. They claim that the individual Israelites in these descriptive passages may have been innocent of a particular sin, but still shared in the guilt of their nation's leniency toward widespread sinful practices, often over multiple generations. For this reason, the prophets repented for the sins of their ancestors and nation. Dr. Tony Evans makes this argument in *Oneness Embraced*.

> We see this biblical model in the books of Daniel and Nehemiah where both prophets repented on behalf of their people. While doing so, both prophets included themselves personally in the prayer of repentance even though there is no indication that either prophet participated in the sin itself (Daniel 9:5, 7; Nehemiah 1:6-7). Thus, personal repentance on behalf of corporate sin that led to any degree of impact, benefit, or privilege for the corporate body ought to be offered in a like manner of sincere humility.[6]

Racial reconciliation advocates then connect this principle to the American context. Even though no white Americans today directly participated in the sin of slavery and may not have had ancestors who did, they still bear some level of guilt. Because white people belong to the same "corporate body" of those who did participate in racial injustice, they need to engage in corporate repentance on behalf of the guilty.

Another common argument is that since all humans bear the stain of our ancestor Adam's sin, it's possible for an ethnic group or a nation to bear the stains of their ancestors. Just as we inherited Adam's guilt even though we didn't participate in his original sin, we also bear the guilt of other ancestors. Joshua 7 tells us Achan's family was put to death even though the text doesn't specify whether they participated in his sin of theft. Racial reconciliation advocates then connect this idea to our modern context, saying white people can take corporate responsibility for our ancestors' sins, such as slavery, lynching, Jim Crow laws, redlining practices, and so on. Pastor and Gospel Coalition cofounder Tim Keller seemed fond of this approach. In a popular speech Keller gave at an event launching John Piper's 2012 book *Bloodlines*, he said:

> At the very, very heart of the Bible, at the heart of theology, not just what the Bible says about you and your family, not just what the Bible says about you and your culture, but what the Bible says about you and the human race—how sin happens, how salvation happens—there's corporate responsibility. You got that? If you don't understand that, to some degree, Western people—and white people in particular—don't realize to what degree they filter out all kinds of things the Bible says. They just don't see them, or they resist them because of that individualism. It's not biblical. It's not Gospel.[7]

Keller believed white people are obligated to accept corporate responsibility for the sins of previous generations. In his belief, that principle lies at the very core of our faith.

The third argument for corporate responsibility rests on the idea that people of European descent have inherited, and still benefit from, unearned advantages (white privilege, wealth) as a result of historic injustices done to slaves and their descendants. For this reason, they are complicit in racism and participating in racist systems, even if they aren't actively racist themselves. This guilt requires confession and repentance.

Each approach to making the case for corporate guilt and repentance has a kernel of truth. This makes navigating the arguments and responding to them a bit tricky.

Evaluating National Repentance

Christians generally agree we will be held accountable for our individual sins. In fact, God's law specifically states, "Fathers shall not be put to death because of their children, nor shall children be put to death because of their fathers. Each one shall be put to death for his own sin" (Deuteronomy 24:16; see also Ezekiel 18:2-4, 20). This law is a reflection of God's justice standard. Someday, every human being will stand before God to be judged for our actions (Revelation 20:11-15). We will not be held accountable for the sins of our fathers or our children, except those that we have directly participated in. Those who have trusted Christ and had their names written in the book of life will enter the new heavens and new earth (Revelation 21–22). Those whose names are not will enter the lake of fire created for the devil and his cohorts. Both the racial reconciliation model and the biblical unity model agree on these points.

The key question of dispute between the models is whether national or corporate repentance is a biblically supported concept. Can individuals repent for the sins of others, including previous generations? Repentance should not be confused with the modern practice of saying a hollow "I apologize" to smooth over a difficult situation. Rather, the biblical concept of repentance begins with a changing of the mind and heart and then expresses itself through words and changed behavior. It involves going in a new direction. Repentance also requires an acknowledgement that the sins are committed against the Creator (Nehemiah 1:6; Luke 15:18). This is work that only an individual can do.

For many years, Monique was unaware of how she engaged in rough thoughts about "all white people." Once the Holy Spirit brought these matters to her awareness, she repented of these thoughts and worked to cooperate with the Holy Spirit to become more conformed to the image of Christ in how she thought about people of other ethnicities. This work of repentance is something only she can do.

Even if we had nothing directly to do with their sin, we can, however, acknowledge the sins of others. When we encounter someone who has experienced a horrible injustice, we can be a generous listener and provide comfort and empathy. On one occasion, my husband was attempting to share the gospel with a young woman in a street evangelism situation. She explained that one of her barriers to faith was that she had been horribly abused by her father. My husband patiently listened to her and then "stood in" for her unrepentant father and said, "I'm sorry that happened to you." He prayed with her for healing and shared the gospel with her. He acknowledged the sin, and expressed sympathy for her experience, but he could not directly repent for the sin of her father. Acknowledging the sins of others, along with their impacts, can be a way of extending compassion to an injured party. We might even be able to step in and offer a level of repair to the situation. But we should also be aware that these steps are not the same as repentance.

Another step we can take is to *renounce* the unjust acts of others, such as the leaders of our nation, both past and present. We can demonstrate our distance from these wicked acts by working to advance legislation to correct current injustices or prevent past injustices from reoccurring. If possible, we might also be able to address the impacts of these injustices.

When we see Nehemiah or Daniel interceding on behalf of their nation, racial reconciliation advocates are right to draw our attention to the use of the first person, even though we don't know to what degree they directly participated in these sins.

> As soon as I heard these words I sat down and wept and mourned for days, and I continued fasting and praying before the God of heaven. And I said, "O LORD God of heaven, the great and awesome God who keeps covenant and steadfast love with those who love him and keep his commandments, let your ear be attentive and your eyes open, to hear the prayer of your servant that I now pray before you day and night for the people of Israel your servants, confessing the sins of the people of Israel, which *we have sinned against you.* Even I and my father's house have sinned. We have acted very corruptly against you and have not kept the commandments, the statutes, and the rules that you commanded your servant Moses" (Nehemiah 1:4-7).

Both Nehemiah and Daniel acknowledge the sins of previous and current generations (Daniel 9:1-19). Both include themselves in the "we" who have broken God's commandments. Both appeal to God's mercy and love on behalf of their nation. But neither prophet could truly repent in the strictest sense of the word on behalf of others. Why? Because repentance is something that individuals must do.

We also have a few examples in Scripture where we see leaders repent of the sins of previous generations and turn back to God (such as King Josiah, 2 Kings 22:2, 11, 19). Then they led their people into destroying idols and called them to renew their commitment to God (2 Kings 23). Even the Assyrian capital of Nineveh turned away God's wrath through their repentance (Jonah 3:5-10). But those efforts started with repentance in the leadership first and then trickled down to the citizens.

As Christians, we can repent of our own sins, call others to repentance (like our governmental leaders), and we can acknowledge and renounce the sins of others. We can also follow the examples of Daniel and Nehemiah and pray for our people, ask the Lord for mercy, call out the sins of our nation, and participate in efforts to revive knowledge about the Word of God. We can rejoice when our nation turns away from unjust laws and replaces them with laws that are more consistent with God's justice standards.

But racial reconciliation advocates go far beyond this. Their vision for corporate repentance requires all white people to acknowledge their ancestors' participation, even their own unintentional participation. It involves dismantling what they see as racist systems and structures that inherently advantage white people. Until racial disparities are ended in education, the prison systems, and we (white people) are advocating for these causes around our own dinner tables, then in their minds corporate repentance hasn't even begun. The problem is, most of the time, these so-called "sins" are identified through the lens of sociology and without a clear warrant in Scripture, and their cure is entirely man-made. This is not the picture of repenting to the God of heaven for the sins outlined in His Word.

At the final judgment, every individual will be held accountable for their own deeds, not their failure to repent for the sins of others or their nation's past sins (Matthew 12:36; Romans 14:12; 1 Peter 4:5). In the meantime, while we are awaiting the final judgment, Christians—especially Christian leaders, regardless of ethnicity—have an obligation to speak out against national injustices that violate God's moral law. Christians don't sit idly by and keep silent about the sins of their nation.

There's No Such Thing as Racial Federal Headship

Much of the case for racial reconciliation rests on a faulty analogy between ancient Israel and "white people." Here's the problem: There is no biblical evidence that God has a covenant relationship with any group of people based on ethnicity, outside of the descendants of Jacob. He doesn't have a covenantal relationship with "white people" any more than He has a covenantal relationship with Asian people, Africans, Americans, or Jamaicans. Arguments for corporate guilt based in federal headship are similarly flawed. Advocates of this idea, like Tim Keller, extrapolate the idea of corporate racial guilt from the transmission of original sin and the imputation of Christ's righteousness. Federal headship contains the idea that Adam and Jesus (called the second Adam based on Romans 5:14) act as representatives on behalf of all humanity; therefore, white people can act as representatives who repent on behalf of their race.[8]

But as the first human being and the Son of God, Adam and Jesus each had unique and particular roles in redemptive history; one brought sin into the world, and the other paid the price for it so we as individuals no longer have to. There isn't warrant to apply that principle of federal headship to other individuals or groups. Just as God doesn't have a covenant with white people, neither is there a federal head of white people or a federal head for descendants of African slaves. According to Romans 5, there are two—and only two—federal heads. All humans are either "in Christ" or "in Adam." In short, supporting reparations by appealing to the headship of Adam is simply bad exegesis.

My skepticism about whether corporate repentance can be biblically substantiated doesn't mean that I don't believe that the sinful behaviors or beliefs of previous generations have no connection to our current cultural moment. The actions of those who came before us set events in motion that can cause social chaos, even if we played no direct role in creating the current situation. It's true that individual Christians sometimes fail to obey the law of Christ. Some Christians did participate in the slave trade, and some Christian leaders advanced flawed "biblical" arguments to support the American slave trade and racial hierarchies. Some Christians failed to speak up on behalf of the exploited. But it's also true that others did speak up. Some did fight against slavery. Some paid with their lives. But what Christians must do in *this* moment is confess and repent of their *personal* sins. And even if we suffer from the consequences of other people's sins, the first responsibility of all true disciples of Jesus—not just white Christians—is to obey God's Word. Each of us will be held accountable for the way of life we choose.

A WAY FORWARD

Monique and I have walked a lot of miles in our individual journeys on the issue of reparations. Monique doesn't advocate for national reparations anymore, but she does wish our country's government would at least issue a national apology for its participation in slavery. Even so, she can still get emotional when she's trying to have a discussion about historical accuracy and the other person refuses to listen.

I'm able to have the discussion now and be a better listener without simply being reactive. But I'll admit, it's still emotional at times. The constant rhetoric in our culture to villainize white people, question our motives, denigrate our culture, and mock our behaviors is often exhausting. Sometimes it makes me want to check out of the discussion. So I always appreciate it when Monique checks in with me and says, "I know it's kind of rough to be white today. How are you doing?"

Moving forward together has meant learning how to deal with the person in front of us, and not turning each other into avatars for our ancestors. Our hope is that Christians on both sides of the discussion will make better biblical arguments and listen more generously to one another. We also hope Christians won't just sit around bickering about reparations or waiting for the government to take action. We must be distinctly Christian in how we participate in this discussion.

Look, the world is going to be crazy. Who knows? Reparations may lead to a civil war in our country. But even if that happens, it won't change the fact that Christians are called out from among their respective cultures to be ambassadors of God's kingdom. Even if you think the man next to you in church is a "barbarian" (Colossians 3:11), once you are both in Christ, you are family. And you must follow the Father's household rules and learn how to get along and love one another. You'll have to move past your prejudices about "barbarians" and train your mind to no longer think about him according to a worldly point of view (2 Corinthians 5:16).

There are temptations to sin on both sides of the discussion. It's easy for all of us to fall into bitterness, anger, coveting, and resentment. But the Father calls all His children to practice patience, forgiveness, repentance, generous listening, and unbiased investigation of the evidence, and to rejoice in the truth.

If you struggle with resentment or bitterness when the topic of reparations comes up, especially because you believe the "other side" keeps advancing ideas that advocate injustice, ask the Holy Spirit to reveal *His* truth about your heart and where it needs to change.

If you struggle with lack of patience with a friend from a different ethnicity when this topic comes up, this might be God's opportunity to help you grow in the fruit of the Spirit.

If you find yourself thinking cynical thoughts about the other person's pain or tears, it's probably time to stop talking and practice better listening skills.

I think it's also worth noting that some of the people who were directly impacted by Jim Crow laws or redlining practices are still alive. Rather than advocate for an unjust forced government wealth redistribution program (which may violate biblical prohibitions against theft), we believe the ideal situation would be for Christians to follow the biblical pattern of person-to-person restoration. Perhaps local churches can find ways to facilitate restitution for those particular victims, especially those who live in their area. Maybe a former shopkeeper who once enforced Jim Crow bathroom policies or a banker who used to participate in redlining could look for a way to apologize and potentially compensate his neighbors who were wronged.

We recognize that trying to correct these injustices 60 years later could be very challenging. But since some of these people are still alive, why shouldn't some effort be made? Our hope is that Christians will ask the Holy Spirit if there is anything He would have us do, either as individuals or as churches. Perhaps your family came into wealth due directly to slavery, or you own land that once housed slaves. Ask the Lord if He wants you to do anything about that. Maybe He does, maybe He doesn't. We aren't here to arbitrate that. But if He does put something on your heart, obey Him.

Distinctly biblical restitution efforts are motivated by love and are accomplished between individuals. While most Christians may not have done anything that requires biblical restitution, all of us can ask God how to participate in modeling His grace and generosity to others. We can ask God to move the hearts of Christians to consider how to help descendants of slaves start businesses, access better educational options, and advocate for two-parent families. This would provide genuine opportunities to uplift many from poverty. Best of all, it would be driven by love.

REFLECTION QUESTIONS

1. Prior to reading this chapter, what did you think about the concept of paying reparations to black Americans? How did this chapter affect your thoughts on this subject?

2. From a biblical perspective, how do you define *restoration*? How does person-to-person restoration differ from the world's ideas of reparations programs? What are some examples of scenarios when person-to-person restoration might be the best course of action?

3. What thoughts do you have about the concept of corporate repentance? To what extent did this chapter change your understanding of this concept?

4. What steps can you take to become a better listener and less reactive? What can help you overcome the temptation to be reactive rather than hear the other person out first?

5. In what practical ways can you model Christlike generosity and grace to others?

CHAPTER 9

SHOULD ALL CHURCHES BE MULTIETHNIC?

Krista Bontrager

onique's journey with Christ began shortly before her sixteenth birthday, when a new friend invited her to go to a "teen club." That sounded great to Monique. She had always wanted to go to a club. They met at the end of her street and walked three blocks to a church around the corner.

"A church?!"

Not what Monique had in mind.

She was wearing club clothes, not church clothes. Her friend explained the name of her youth group was Club EM. Every Wednesday night, about 150 junior and senior high kids from the local schools showed up to play games, dance, and hear a message about Jesus. But it was mainly the dancing, games, and prizes that kept everyone coming back.

The church was located in a once-affluent community in the heart of North Hollywood. The neighborhood demographics were mixed, but the church's leadership and core membership were predominantly white. As the socioeconomic factors of the community had shifted over time, church members moved farther away and drove in for church on Sundays. But the youth pastor had a vision to build a youth group that reflected the surrounding community. The division in the church was real. Students came from a different generation than the church's core membership, as well as a different culture. One Sunday morning, Monique walked down a hallway and passed two elderly white women. The women clutched their handbags and huddled together as she walked by, causing her to think, *This is why black and white folks don't go to church together. They don't trust us.*

But that was a two-way street. When Monique first started attending the group, her mother warned her sternly about going to a white church. In her mother's mind, going to a black church was fine, but going to church with white people was different. "Kiki," she said, "white people are touchy-feely. Don't you let those white people hug all up on you. You understand me?"

Over time, the church did become more reflective of the community, but not without some growing pains. Most of the older generation who liked things "as they were" left. Meanwhile, Monique still struggled with her mother's comments about "that white church."

Experiences like this proved in her mind that Dr. Martin Luther King Jr.'s words from 1960 were still just as true in 1993: "It is appalling that the most segregated hour of Christian America is eleven o'clock on Sunday morning."[1] This, along with her later worship experiences at Biola University, also birthed a vision in her heart that she would often repeat to me on our walks in the early months of our friendship: "Every church should be multiethnic. The leadership and the congregation should look like the United Nations, with everyone singing and waving flags in worship together."

Monique's stories made me reflect deeply on aspects of local church life I hadn't given much thought to before we became friends. I could see her point. Looking at the numbers, there are a lot of predominantly white churches. Was this "segregation" a result of racism? Or was it something else?

THE MOVEMENT TOWARD
MULTIETHNIC CHURCHES

A multiethnic church really is a beautiful vision. Sadly, our country has a rough history when it comes to church segregation. In a very real sense, the black church was born because of the sin of racism.

The African Methodist Episcopal (AME) Church was established in 1787 by Richard Allen and Absalom Jones. Allen and Jones, preachers at St. George's Episcopal Church in Philadelphia, were only allowed to preach sermons to black congregants. One sanitized version of the story says that they left the church due to discrimination.[2] Allen's version says their departure was forced when white church officials pulled praying black congregants off their knees during a service. Allen and more than 40 others left the church. Either way, the black church was born.[3]

Historically, the black church has provided a stabilizing force in the African American community, serving as a hub for spiritual growth, fellowship, culture, professional networking, and activism. Sadly, as we've mentioned, some black pastors borrow heavily from both black liberation theology and the Word of Faith movement. Both have damaged black churches and black culture.

While white and black churches remained separate throughout much of American history, recent years have brought big changes, especially in predominantly white evangelical churches. Over the last three decades, Duke Divinity School professor Mark Chaves has tracked an upward trend in racial and ethnic diversity in these churches.[4] In 1998, only 7 percent of US evangelical congregations were multiracial ("multiracial" meaning that no one racial or ethnic group constituted more than 80 percent of the congregation's participants). While racially diverse evangelical congregations were still the minority in 2019, the number had risen to 22 percent of churches and was steadily rising. Predominantly white congregations continued to decline. Prior to the 2020 calls for more ethnically diverse churches, predominantly white evangelical churches were already moving in that direction.

Then George Floyd died. Almost overnight, pastors of predominantly white congregations began asking different questions. They started to wonder, *Am I a racist? Is my church racist? Do I need to fix something?* The culture, as well as some voices in trusted evangelical institutions, insisted that the existence of predominantly white congregations staffed by predominantly white leaders signified systemic racism. But is this actually true?

THE CHURCH IS ALREADY MULTIETHNIC

When Monique and I are on consulting calls with pastors, one of our standard questions is: Do you think every church should be multiethnic? They usually respond with a quick and unqualified *yes.*

A 2021 Lifeway phone survey of a thousand senior or lead pastors yielded similar results: 88 percent said that "every church should strive to achieve racial diversity."[5] Yet 76 percent of the respondents said their church consisted primarily of one racial or ethnic group. Our theory is that strong social conditioning, especially in the last few years, has led many to believe that a multiethnic church is the ideal and that every predominantly white church needs to transition into being a multiethnic church to avoid being racist. That's a lot of pressure, especially if you are a pastor in, say, rural Wyoming, where the minority population is likely in the single digits to begin with.

When we ask pastors *why* they believe this, they usually say something like, "Because there are representatives from 'every nation, tribe, and language' worshiping at the throne in heaven, every church should reflect that ideal."

But here's the problem. Revelation 7:9-10 doesn't describe a *local* church. In context, Revelation 7 is describing the universal, global church worshiping together in the throne room of heaven. It's a snapshot not only of what *will happen* in the future, but of the reality that is *happening right now and has been happening* from the beginning of the church. Jesus's final instructions to His disciples were to preach the gospel and disciple the nations (Matthew 28:18-20). Since Pentecost, Christianity *has been* a multiethnic religion. Notice the variety of people groups represented by the diasporic Jews gathered in Jerusalem on that day:

> Now there were dwelling in Jerusalem Jews, devout men from every nation under heaven....Parthians and Medes and Elamites and residents of Mesopotamia, Judea and Cappadocia, Pontus and Asia, Phrygia and Pamphylia, Egypt and the parts of Libya belonging to Cyrene, and visitors from Rome, both Jews and proselytes, Cretans and Arabians—we hear them telling in our own tongues the mighty works of God....So those who received his word were baptized, and there were added that day about three thousand souls (Acts 2:5, 9-11, 41).

In that moment, the gospel exploded into multiple languages and ethnic populations. The opportunity to reach so many ethnic groups with the gospel all at once, combined with the availability of a complex system of Roman roads during a time of relative peace, helped facilitate the rapid spread of the good news throughout the Roman Empire. By the end of the book of Acts, the gospel had spread to North Africa, Asia, and into Europe.

From both a global and historical perspective, the church is already multiethnic, multicultural, and multilingual. No matter where you go in the world, you are likely to find authentic Christians. There might be fewer of them in some areas, and some unreached people groups still need Bibles in their language. But in general, the gospel has gone out to the nations. Revelation 7 is the confirmation that Matthew 28:19-20 is already a reality—one that will only continue to grow until the Lord's return. Having every local church be multi-ethnic isn't the goal; a global multiethnic church is already our reality.

HOW TO FIND OUT IF
YOUR CHURCH IS RACIST

No patient would want a doctor to diagnose an illness and initiate drastic treatments without first conducting some thorough tests. So why would we want to diagnose and treat a church's condition without carefully examining the symptoms and their source? As Monique explained previously, disparities don't automatically serve as proof of systemic racism. Evidence is needed to confirm whether a particular disparity is caused by racial biases. Accusations don't automatically equal truth. We need to carefully investigate in order to correctly diagnose a situation before we attempt to treat it.

Is there something defective about my church if it's mostly white? This question lingers in the back of many white pastors' minds, often unspoken. And it's understandable. Again, social pressure and conditioning, especially since 2020, means that something is wrong if most of the people in the room are white.

The truth is, it *might* be sinful. It *might* be racist. And it might *not* be.

A correct diagnosis requires asking the right questions. The first step is to assess a church's context. The most basic question Monique and I encourage a leadership team to ask is: Does your church or school generally reflect the demographics of the surrounding community?

Leadership will need to gather some data about the makeup of the community within a certain radius, say within roughly five miles of the church building. For a Christian school, studying the community within a 15-mile radius may be more helpful. Church or school leaders can enter the organization's zip code into the US Census Bureau's website and retrieve data about the surrounding community's racial makeup, dominant languages, socioeconomic status, and even religious beliefs. For designing outreach to these communities, it may also be helpful to look up data about living conditions (rentals versus home ownership), family demographics (single versus married), and how many people own computers and have internet access. Gathering this data will help build an accurate picture of the demographics most likely within reach of your church or school. If the organization is a good representation of the surrounding community, then there might not be a problem with racism, even if your church is predominantly white.

But what if your church does not appear to reflect the surrounding community? Well, it's time to explore why that's the case. Start by investigating possible blind spots. Ask these questions:

- Is there a lack of hospitality toward outsiders who visit our church?

- Have we taken steps to let the community know about our church?

- Is the leadership or the congregation apathetic about reaching particular groups in the neighborhood with the gospel?

- Is the distance between the community and the church the result of a previously undetected oversight?

Church leaders may need to develop new strategies to take the gospel to those living nearby. But this must be done out of a conviction to bring the gospel to a community, not merely a desire to reach "diversity goals." The purpose of the church is to bring the gospel to all the nations, not to achieve a certain demographic makeup.

WHEN MULTIETHNIC
LEADERSHIP MATTERS

White pastors often wonder if their church is racist if they haven't hired minority staff members. Of course, turning down a qualified candidate simply because of skin color or because a congregation isn't "ready" for a minority pastor would be participating in unbiblical racial partiality. But when white pastors reach out to us with questions about church leadership diversity, their concern usually stems from the belief that racial disparities in leadership amount to systemic racism. It is not uncommon for racial reconciliation advocates to tell white pastors they must correct the "power dynamics" of leadership by intentionally hiring minority staff members. We've had pastors ask us how to transition to multiethnic leadership so they can "fix" this perceived power problem. Because the church is racist if the leadership is monoethnic, right? Not necessarily.

Typical diversity hiring has multiple pitfalls and often runs counter to biblical guidelines for choosing leaders. Two influential evangelical pastors, Dr. Eric Mason and Pastor Matt Chandler, demonstrated some of these pitfalls at the MLK50 conference (sponsored by the Gospel Coalition) in January 2019. During this event, Chandler decried "tokenism," the practice of hiring unqualified candidates for positions based simply on their minority status.[6] But just a few minutes later, Chandler shared that he "called every African American man" he knew asking for names of black candidates to fill a position leading a two-thousand-member congregation with an 11-million-dollar budget. When he also hired a recruiting firm to look for more candidates, the firm asked him: "If we find an Anglo eight and an African American seven, which one do you want?" Chandler replied, "I want the African American seven."[7] While Chandler insists on not hiring a less-qualified candidate simply because that person is black, he appears to have attempted to do just that for the sake of achieving skin-color diversity.

We believe this approach is mistaken. The Bible lays out clear qualifications for church leadership, and ethnicity is not among them.

In a different talk at the same conference, Mason argued that some black hires are "not qualified" because of something similar to what racial reconciliation advocates call "internalized whiteness" or "internalized racism." He said,

> [White people] need to begin to educate yourself on beginning to develop the opportunity to not have reductionist ways in which you try to cause racial reconciliation, like through hiring nonqualified African-Americans to be the multiethnic engineers in your local churches. And you know they're not qualified because blacks haven't hired them. And it works against unity when you hire somebody that we not feeling, and you're wondering why multiethnicity isn't happening at your church. It's because you have a person that's *black on the outside but Angloid on the inside.*[8]

Essentially, Mason argues that someone who is considered racially black but culturally white hinders achieving ethnic diversity in the church.

As for his choice of words, Monique and I believe calling a black person "Angloid on the inside" is a racial slur, similar to calling a black person an "Oreo" or a "coon." These slurs, considered degrading insults in the black community, reflect the idea that some people are "skin folk" but not "kinfolk" and reinforce the myth of racialization, namely that skin color ought to determine culture or ideology. Suffice it to say, it ought not be heard in the church.

While we disagree with Mason's choice of words, he does make a point worth considering: Sometimes having a leader with inside knowledge of a specific culture can be helpful, especially when a particular community needs servicing. Sometimes the current leadership can't reach it due to cultural or language barriers.

In these cases, having qualified, spiritually mature, culturally native church leaders on staff could enable churches to reach their communities with the gospel. But this is ultimately a matter of culture, not race. As Mason said, shared skin color is not the same as shared culture. If an inner-city church in Los Angeles hires an African American man from rural Alabama, they may discover he lacks the skills to connect with an urban community. The same might also be true of an African American who was adopted by a white family or of a Nigerian pastor who immigrated to inner-city Chicago. But a white candidate who grew up in China may be the perfect addition to a church staff trying to reach Chinese immigrants.

The cultural distance, even among those who look similar, can be significant. In addition, skin tone does not indicate theological or ideological sameness or soundness. If a theologically conservative church of any ethnicity hired a pastor influenced by liberation theology or progressive teachings, that could be catastrophic.

If leaders make skin tone a primary consideration, churches may miss opportunities to see the gospel spread in "outside the box" ways. Our friend Marcus is an African American man who pastors a Chinese church. On the outside, he might not look like the best candidate, but Marcus lived in China for several years and has a deep understanding of the culture. He is also a man of God who lives out the ideals of biblical unity. He's well suited to the task. In cases where a church has culture-specific hiring needs, the search can and should concentrate on finding the most theologically and culturally qualified candidate for effective outreach.

CHOOSING THE RIGHT LEADERS

When Paul commissioned Titus to appoint elders to lead the church in Crete, he provided very specific criteria for what qualified a person to lead:

> This is why I left you in Crete, so that you might put what remained into order, and appoint elders in every town as I directed you—if anyone is above reproach, the husband of one wife, and his children are believers and not open to the charge of debauchery or insubordination. For an overseer, as God's steward, must be above reproach. He must not be arrogant or quick-tempered or a drunkard or violent or greedy for gain, but hospitable, a lover of good, self-controlled, upright, holy, and disciplined. He must hold firm to the trustworthy word as taught, so that he may be able to give instruction in sound doctrine and also to rebuke those who contradict it (Titus 1:5-9).

Paul gave similar instructions to Timothy for the Ephesian church in 1 Timothy 3:1-7. These guidelines aren't merely Paul's opinion; they are the Lord's *prescriptions* for appointing church leadership. Character and spiritual maturity come first. Paul does not mention recruiting elders based on ethnicity, skin tone, culture, or regional origin. So, we must be careful about vaulting skin color, a standard God doesn't require, over the pole labeled "vital job requirement."

In the book of Acts, Luke provides *descriptive* examples of this principle of qualified spiritual leadership. While racial reconciliation advocates often leverage Acts 6:1-6 to call for reorganizing power structures in the local church, as Monique mentioned earlier, we don't find that application convincing. Still, while Luke doesn't explicitly say that ethnicity or culture were requirements in the deacons' recruiting, it *may* have been a consideration. Whether it was or not, the passage is clear that those recruited must meet the criteria for godly leadership first. We aren't told that the men chosen in Acts 6 were promoted into leadership simply because of their ethnicity. They were *first and foremost* men of sound doctrine and righteous living.

Luke indicates in Acts 13:1-3 that the leadership in the church in Antioch was organically multiethnic. But this multicultural and multiethnic leadership wasn't the result of a calculated campaign to even out power dynamics. It was the natural outworking of the Holy Spirit and evidence of the spread of the gospel that began at Pentecost. For this reason, we strongly caution churches against recruiting elders and staff members simply to meet "diversity goals." Worldly diversity standards are an inappropriate form of ethnic partiality. Instead, we encourage church leaders to focus on strategic, gospel-centered ministry and let diversity develop organically. While best practices in missions, evangelism, and discipleship tell us that outreach is often most effective when done by cultural natives, keep in mind that God can still work through those who are not. God has moved the gospel across vast cultural and linguistic boundaries through men and women like Hudson Taylor and Jim and Elisabeth Elliot. All He needs are willing followers. If He is leading the effort, He will make a way.

WHEN DO ETHNICITY, CULTURE, OR LANGUAGE MATTER?

As the Western world becomes more multiethnic, churches may experience a greater need to engage in multicultural or multilingual ministry. If a church sees a deficiency in its ability to reach or disciple a particular community, that's the time to look for qualified leaders who also have the needed linguistic or cultural skills.

Making Room for Multilingual Ministry

Revelation 7 describes people speaking every language worshiping around God's throne. As beautiful as that vision is, language differences can be a very real barrier in ministry. If the gospel is to reach "every nation" (v. 9), it must cross linguistic barriers to get there. Some churches have introduced multilingual services or added other-language services to meet their communities' needs. Many, however, do not have accommodations for other languages. To be clear, there is nothing inherently wrong or racist about having a monoethnic church that only worships in one language. A Chinese-speaking church, for example, is not being sinfully ethnocentric if they hold services in only Mandarin. Still, adding another language service or transitioning to bilingual services can be helpful, especially when the cultural makeup of the neighborhood around a church begins to change.

In the mid-1980s, my predominantly white church saw a steady increase of Spanish-speaking residents in the surrounding neighborhood, so the elders laid out their vision to launch a Spanish-speaking church. The church would recruit and pay a full-time Spanish-speaking pastor and would also commission five bilingual families from our church to provide a stable core for the new congregation. The elders identified couples who had attended our church for over a decade, were mature in the Lord, embedded in the target culture, spoke the language, and had appropriate spiritual gifts to spearhead the outreach.

The church's financial, relational, and spiritual investment in the new congregation spread the gospel to new members of the community. These investments made the Spanish-speaking service an organic part of the church from the beginning. Children from both services attended Sunday school and youth groups together, families got to know each other, and the church sponsored activities a couple times a year to bring everyone together. This wasn't simply a Spanish-speaking congregation renting our facilities; we were one church and one family.

If a church hasn't been reaching out to other ethnic or cultural groups in the surrounding community, probe why that might be the case. There might be prejudice at play, or it might simply be an oversight. A majority white, English-speaking church located in an 80-percent Spanish-speaking neighborhood that hasn't actively engaged in gospel outreach or actively trained godly Spanish-speaking men for leadership might need to explore what it would take to disciple or recruit qualified men for future leadership. Likewise, a Chinese church whose surrounding community has seen a sharp increase in Farsi-speaking immigrants might need to begin praying for the Lord to send a qualified Farsi-speaking Christian to join the pastoral staff and for God's provision to fund the new Farsi-speaking pastor's salary.

As neighborhoods change, local church elders must be open to thinking creatively about how to reach their surrounding community with the gospel. If church leaders are not willing to shape a vision for doing so, there might be a sin problem. In this case, remaining a monolingual congregation could become a cover for hiding apathy toward non-Christians, or in some cases, hiding antipathy toward another people group.

A healthy church disciples and trains future leaders. When the surrounding community would benefit from culturally fluent leadership, churches will need to seek and train godly men who have the necessary cultural knowledge and skills. This should always be for the sake of spreading the gospel more effectively, not to make the church look more diverse on its website.

Making Room for Multicultural Ministry

Multilingual and multicultural ministry are often intertwined, though not always. Culture can be the source of major differences between people in the same language group. As human beings, we like being with people who are like us. This tendency encompasses all cultures. We prefer to be with those who share the same music, laugh at the same jokes, and understand our lingo.

This was true for me and Monique. Much of the divide between us in the early days of friendship turned out to be cultural, not racial. I didn't understand anything about braids, relaxers (perms that make your hair straight), bonnets, or why the smoke from Monique's hot comb fills the entire house with a particular smell. Meanwhile, Monique was confused by the difference in typical white and black parenting styles. The way we understood each other's tone of voice was different. Our taste in worship music was wildly divergent. The cultural differences and resulting confusion we experienced weren't sinful, they were just matters of providence. Our traditions weren't designed to leave others out; they were simply an expression of our unique cultures.

But not everyone sees it this way. Once, after Monique finished speaking at an event, a group of African American women approached her. For over an hour, she patiently answered their questions. One woman asked, "Why are white churches so racist?" When Monique asked for a specific example, the woman said the music style in many churches was "white." Monique asked, "Well, if a white person came to a black church and we were all singing a particular kind of way that was unfamiliar to them, would that be racism?" The woman responded, "Oh no. That's just our culture."

Exactly. Not all cultural differences are racist.

If we apply the same standard justly and equally to everyone without prejudice, then a white guy strumming a guitar slowly is no more racist than a black guy playing a Hammond organ loudly. It's an expression of cultural differences. As long as they are theologically sound, both styles can have a place in the church. Both can be beautiful, even if you personally prefer one over the other.

In most cases, multiethnic and multicultural churches will require everyone to sacrifice some personal preferences. It is not reasonable or possible for such churches to fully accommodate the cultures of all members. This isn't racist, just reality.

Because of how tightly music is tied to cultural expression, musical preferences are one of the biggest barriers to multiethnic and multicultural churches. Especially in countries where church options abound, this plays a huge role in the decisions people make about the church they attend. Sadly, sometimes preserving these preferences can become more important to a congregation than discipling the church's attendees. Church leaders in multicultural settings might need to think about how their music style can include the whole congregation while maintaining biblically sound worship as the priority. Maybe a mixture of hymns and some modern worship music is needed in order to include people from a wider age range. Perhaps the music director could mix in some black gospel music or other styles. And yes, some churches may need to make room for that guitar guy too!

SHOULD BLACK CHURCHES BECOME MULTIETHNIC?

Typically, the burden for planting an interethnic church is placed squarely on the shoulders of white pastors. We understand why the black church was originally separated out and why it has long remained that way. Still, perhaps it is time for pastors of historically black churches to also develop a vision for interethnic local churches. After all, we personally know many black pastors who also have a heart for the gospel and reaching the lost.

What if a historically black church now sits in a predominantly Hispanic community or one that has become "gentrified" with young white couples? Does that church bear no responsibility for reaching these communities? We ask, respectfully, to what degree are leaders at black churches willing to modify their instrumentation, song selection, or preaching styles for the sake of cross-cultural outreach?

These are powerful, and some might say disturbing, questions. It is possible that a monoethnic church, even a black church, might become a cover for apathy toward the people of a different ethnicity in the name of cultural preservation—something white Christians are almost universally called upon to forsake.

Regardless of ethnicity, may such sins of apathy or antipathy never be tolerated among us.

Creating multiethnic churches isn't necessarily the ideal. The world is a much more complicated place than that. The ultimate goal is to have gospel-focused churches. When we see a monoethnic church, we shouldn't jump to the conclusion that it must be defective, sinful, or less than ideal. It might be, but it might not. Our thinking about the issue of multiethnic churches must be founded on Scripture, not on the whims or pressures of culture. For some church leaders, this approach will provide some relief. For others, it will open new challenges.

REFLECTION QUESTIONS

1. Prior to reading this chapter, what did you think about the concept of multiethnic churches? How did this chapter affect your thoughts on this subject?

2. How do we see God's glory reflected in the multiethnic nature of the body of Christ on a global scale both in the New Testament and today?

3. Does your church reflect the demographics of the building's surrounding community in ethnicity, culture, and socioeconomic status? What do you think your church does well in this area? Where could they improve?

4. What are Scripture's criteria for selecting church elders or pastors? How well does your church follow these criteria? Where could they improve?

5. What is your church doing to raise up and train new leaders from within the congregation in order to preach the gospel to the surrounding community?

CHAPTER 10

WHERE DO MULTIETHNIC FAMILIES FIT IN?

Monique Duson

In the thick of 2020's racial reckoning, we received a message from a young woman asking our opinion about interethnic adoption. She and her husband were becoming foster parents with the hope of eventually adopting. But after seeing negative comments on social media about interethnic adoption, she was having second thoughts. Her friends were claiming that black children are damaged when white people adopt them.

Rather than write her back, Krista and I took a walk one evening and called her on the phone. The woman explained that she and her husband had struggled with infertility. They wanted to give a foster child a good home, but she was growing concerned that by potentially adopting a child of a different ethnicity, they would be participating in colonization.

This woman's experience and self-doubt aren't unusual. Many interethnic families face complex challenges, as do many biracial families when the culture demands that their children "pick a side." Some antiracists decry interethnic adoption and discourage interethnic marriages. Families feel pressured, and their children are often left feeling uncertain about their core identity and which culture to affirm.

Our nation's ethnic identity culture war affects multiethnic families differently than most monoethnic families. Even so, God's Word provides some answers and a place for multiethnic families to belong.

GOD'S DEFINITION OF FAMILY

Since a member of the British royalty has now married a mixed-race woman from Los Angeles, it's hard to imagine that some people are still uncomfortable with interethnic marriage. After all, the US Supreme Court decision in *Loving v. Virginia* enshrined protections for interethnic marriage in 1967. Many chalk up this decision and subsequent social acceptance of interethnic marriage to "progress" or moral evolution. But modern acceptance of interethnic marriage isn't the product of progressivism; it's rooted in the Christian worldview. While it's true that a tiny fraction of misguided Christians still use out-of-context Scripture to argue against marrying outside one's ethnicity, this is not the historic position of our faith. Christianity provides a strong theological foundation for interethnic and intercultural marriage, which rests on three core ideas:

- All people are united by a common humanity.

- The Bible teaches that there is only one human race.

- All humans share two common ancestors: Adam and Eve (see Genesis 1:26-27; 3:20; Acts 17:26).

As members of the family of God, Christians form a new subgroup of humanity. In Christ, ethnic and social differences cease to be obstacles to deep, personal, intimate fellowship between believers.

The Bible's key stipulation for choosing a qualified spouse is that a Christian ought to only marry another Christian (2 Corinthians 6:14).[1] Paul reaffirms the Mosaic law's prohibitions against intermarriage with those outside the covenant. Some have misconstrued the Mosaic law or other Old Testament passages as teaching against interethnic marriages, but the issue in the Old Testament was spiritual, not ethnic. This was a matter of faith and allegiance to the one true God. The Bible doesn't forbid marriage between members of different ethnic, cultural, or even socioeconomic groups because of these factors, but it clearly forbids marriage between members of different spiritual groups. A spouse who is "in Christ" and a spouse who is still "in Adam" are walking in different directions. God's primary concern regarding marriage and procreation is that both spouses be genuine and committed followers of Jesus. Followers of God are to marry and raise their children within the covenant.

Interethnic or intercultural marriages still have their challenges, even when both spouses are under the covenant. Couples may have to navigate language barriers or cultural distance between their families. For some, this might be a bit like living in the film *My Big Fat Greek Wedding* every day! In addition to these challenges, couples will face the reality of living in a sinful world. But if both are willing to submit to the ways of God and endure and overcome those challenges with one another, they ought to be supported and cheered on by their friends and family in the church.

When couples from diverse backgrounds come together, they display the reality of Jesus's work on the cross as the great unifier of His people. A Christian interethnic or intercultural family provides an earthly picture of the new creation in which members of every nation, tribe, and tongue will worship the Lamb. And that's a beautiful thing.

NAVIGATING MULTIETHNIC PARENTING

Our friend Marie is black. She grew up in a very Afrocentric home in a moderately diverse neighborhood. Much like me, she was raised to be proud of her brown skin and ethnic heritage. And she raised her children to be the same.

Marie's husband, Chris, is biracial. His father emigrated to America from China. His mother is a white Midwesterner. (Three of Marie's four siblings married outside their ethnicity, so no one was surprised when she brought home a half-white, half-Asian boyfriend.) That means Marie's biological children are triracial: Chinese, black, and white. They also have a son they adopted from China.

When people look at their family, they usually have some questions. Everyone has different skin colors, hair textures, and facial features. Marie likes to say, "We don't match, and that's okay."

But while her family was fairly accepting, Chris's family struggled. In Chinese culture, it is commonly understood that you don't marry someone with darker skin. Though they have a strong relationship today, Chris's father needed time to adjust to the idea of his son marrying a black woman.

Since 2020, racial tensions within Marie's extended family have become more visible. She and Chris have had to tackle some tough conversations with family members, including addressing degrading statements made about white people. Sadly, these comments have continued, and Marie and her family have distanced themselves from certain members of their extended family. They made the hard decision to model for their children that you can love someone and yet not allow them to degrade you or your loved ones because of skin color or ethnic heritage.

Raising a multiethnic family in a race-obsessed culture means having intentional conversations about things like creation identity, salvation identity, and matters of providence. For Christians, this means first teaching children that all people are created in God's image with equal dignity, value, and worth—regardless of their skin color. Marie and Chris often discuss their ethnic heritage with their children as being a matter of providence: It's something they can celebrate together, but they also make it very clear that ethnic heritage is not their primary identity. For interethnic and intercultural families, it is vital to continually reinforce children's primary identity—their creation and salvation identities.

Christian parents also must model confidence by refusing to cooperate with cultural pressures to demean certain ethnicities. Marie and Chris are pretty fearless. They don't idly sit by in polite conversation while people degrade them or their children. They model kindness while also being direct. Their children have picked up on this, too, building inner confidence so they stand firm and don't let derogatory words shake them. They know who they are.

ANTIRACISM AND ADOPTION

Some families explore adoption due to infertility, while others simply want to offer a loving home to children facing special challenges. Sadly, families who want to adopt children outside their culture or ethnicity often face additional obstacles.

A young adoptive mom approached me a couple of years ago at an event in Pennsylvania. She pointed to a toddler behind her—a small black boy about two years old. "That's my son," she said. "We've had him since he was born, and my husband and I are in the process of adopting."

As a white mom, the woman had been required to sit through antiracism classes before she could adopt a black child. In addition, the adoption agency was sending her messages with suggestions on how to parent a black child. She pulled out her phone and showed me an email she'd received earlier that day. It contained a tip sheet called "How to See Me" with a picture of a young black boy on the front. This deflated young mother wondered: Was she, as a white woman, possibly hurting the child she loved?

That woman is not alone. Hundreds of other adoptive families have asked us the same thing. Antiracism's messaging is clear: Loving and caring for a child well is not enough if you don't share the same skin color. I've noticed, however, that this standard seems to apply only to white parents. Do black or brown foster and adoptive parents of white children receive daily texts about how to help preserve their children's cultural heritage?

Controversy over interethnic marriage and adoption is not new. Beginning in the early 1700s, anti-miscegenation laws restricted sexual relationships between people of different ethnic groups in almost every state. Restrictions were especially designed to prevent white people from intermarrying with other races, encouraging them to see black people as inferior.[2] In addition to creating legal restrictions on interethnic marriages, these laws influenced popular thought about interethnic adoption. Before the civil rights movement, many black children were denied opportunities to be adopted, and interethnic adoption was seen as being potentially harmful to them.[3] Opposition to it began to decrease in the mid-1950s, however, as the United States slowly increased adoptions from countries like Korea and Vietnam in the wake of wars in those countries. Interethnic adoptions of black and Native American children within the US also began to increase. In most cases, the parents most willing or able to open their homes to these children were white. Despite intentional efforts to deracialize the foster care and adoption systems, apprehension over placing black children in white families has lingered, often due to concerns that black children will lose part of their cultural identity. A 1987 *Chicago Tribune* article titled "Should White Parents Be Allowed to Adopt Black Children?" demonstrates this.

The National Association of Black Social Workers has said since 1972 that a black child needs to grow up in a black family to attain a strong racial and personal identity. Dr. Morris Jeff, the association's president and director of city welfare in New Orleans, said his group is interested in preservation of black families and we see the lateral transfer of black children to white families as contradictory to our preservation efforts.[4]

In recent years, antiracists have pushed these claims even further, saying that structures once put in place to help promote the adoption of black children and prevent them from remaining in the child welfare system now perpetuate cultural genocide. Some have accused white parents of colonization,[5] and one progressive Christian influencer went so far as to say she would rather abort a brown baby than let white evangelicals adopt the child.[6] Structures that place black and brown children in white homes, antiracists argue, uphold white supremacy and contribute to the destruction of people of color.

Sadly, the key criteria used for adoption placement is essentially the same as in the late 1940s and early 1950s: the skin color of the child and that of the adoptive family. If white families are approved to adopt interracially, adoption agencies ensure white parents are made aware of how their whiteness will negatively impact children placed in their care. These trainings are supposed to help white parents overcome any implicit biases they may be holding against people of color, including their own children. Here's a sample from the North American Council of Adoptable Children (NACAC):

Because we live in a racialized society where whiteness is the default setting, white experiences and values are often the lens through which white people view the world. Raising a child of color or working in an agency with children of color does not exempt white people from having implicit racist ideologies. This does not make you a bad person. But it does mean you must recognize this fact and be willing to shift that lens. It means you must be unflinching in your stance as an antiracist.[7]

In other words, white parents adopting children of another ethnicity must also adopt an antiracist worldview. The NACAC, a national organization that works alongside adoptive families, isn't simply teaching cross-cultural navigation skills; it's advocating antiracism beliefs and policies. As one core document states, "The placement of children with a family of like ethnic or racial background is preferable because these families have historically demonstrated the ability to equip children with skills and strengths to combat the ill effects of racism."[8] Other stakeholders in the adoption arena echo these sentiments.

While I question these policy recommendations, I am sympathetic to the concerns behind them. Looking at it in the most charitable way, many adoption professionals seem to desire to advocate for children and ensure their cultural identities and practices won't be lost when fostered or adopted by people of a different ethnic heritage. I agree that preserving some cultural heritage and preventing any real mistreatment of children are important goals. My concern is that race-based preferential policies will disadvantage some children, abandoning them in the foster care system simply because there's no match for their cultural or ethnic background. Making issues of secondary importance (race and culture) into issues of primary importance demonstrates how antiracism mixes up our priorities. Racial identity becomes more important than child welfare. Why should any child be denied a safe and stable home when a qualified family of a different ethnicity is ready, willing, and able to love that child through the pain and trauma of a broken past?[9] Antiracism policies of "sharing and learning" in the adoption world appear to be applied only when protecting the identity and cultures of minority children. This implies that the culture and heritage of a white child fostered or adopted by parents of a different ethnicity is, at best, unimportant. Is their cultural heritage to be overlooked or discarded because of their whiteness? The pervasive practice of fusing skin color and culture together contains a troubling assumption that all white people will overlook the ethnic or cultural heritage of the minority child in their care, but that minority parents need not worry about neglecting the heritage and identity needs of white children in their care. I believe that all children, no matter their ethnicity, deserve to have the valuable aspects of their culture celebrated and preserved. That includes white children too. In adoption, as in other areas of life, individual Christians and Christian organizations ought to follow the biblical standard of impartiality.

NAVIGATING MULTIETHNIC ADOPTIVE PARENTING

Multiethnic adoptive families face distinct challenges, but with some wisdom born of past experiences, they can be overcome.

Take Jenny for example. She was born in East Asia, but her culture is Italian-Irish-American. After years of infertility, Jenny's parents chose to adopt her when she was just a few months old. A few years later, her parents finally conceived and gave birth to biological children.

Her parents loved all their kids, but Jenny stuck out. She was an Asian girl growing up in a white family in an all-white suburb. She didn't look like anyone else in her family, her school, or her community. During a census one year, her father joked, "Look, honey, it says that the Asian population is 0.001 percent. That's you!"

Many people today would see his statement as racist, but Jenny says, "My father was not racist. He was a product of the 1970s who tried hard to live according to the tenets of colorblindness." He sought to see Jenny for who she was inside, not for what she looked like on the outside. His joke was meant to be endearing, but it had the unintended consequence of highlighting her as the only Asian in her town. Jenny's parents also didn't understand the impact that the word *Oriental* or jokes about Asian drivers had on her.

Jenny's mom found Eurocentric beauty standards most appealing, often commenting about how she was fond of her own blond hair and blue eyes. As a result, Jenny felt that her dark brown hair and brown eyes didn't measure up. She says that the "unattainable standards of white beauty that were reinforced through dolls, television shows, movies, and my family reminded me that I was different. I struggled with my self-esteem and knowing where I fit in in an all-white society." Aside from one doll given to her by a family friend who visited Jenny's birth country, and the outfit she wore as an infant when she was received by her parents, no part of Jenny's ethnic culture was preserved or passed down.

Growing up, Jenny rarely saw women who looked like her, and was never taught that her Asian features could also be beautiful.

When she became old enough to date, Jenny found herself holding on to the wrong kind of men because they found her beautiful—something she wasn't sure of herself. Even though she grew up in a Christian home and she understood she was created in God's image, today Jenny now believes that seeing more representations of her ethnicity could have helped her feel less alone or abnormal during those years. They could have helped remind her that though the shape of her eyes or the color of her hair were distinct, she didn't need to have blond hair or blue eyes to be beautiful.

Jenny also might have benefited from more guidance in navigating racial stereotypes or negative encounters. She attended predominantly white schools, where she was often seen as the stereotypical "smart Asian" because she excelled scholastically. Some teachers made racial comments, and one even treated her unfairly compared to white children. When she told her parents about these incidents, they didn't know how to handle them—so they did nothing.

Jenny's parents were fairly typical of most adoptive parents 30 years ago. Thankfully, Jenny doesn't hold a grudge against them. She knows they did the best they could with what they knew. She is grateful for her adoption and for God's providence and grace in choosing her family.

Now a parent herself, Jenny understands the challenges of parenting her biracial children. Much like Marie and Chris are doing, she is raising them to understand that their value is not in their physical appearance but in being created in the image of God.

REPRESENTATION: DOES IT REALLY MATTER?

Representation is the idea that when minorities see others like themselves in areas like education, the media, and the arts, they are more apt to envision themselves within those fields. This idea is a key factor in children's toy manufacturers and media companies now producing more black and brown dolls or movie characters. It's also a key factor in why people celebrated the election of the first black US president, Barack Obama, as well as the cultural achievements of other well-known minorities.

When I speak publicly about this issue, I find that most people take one of three positions on the subject. The first group believes representation isn't necessary to believe in one's own abilities or to accomplish great things. They often point to their own experiences as evidence. During a recent Zoom call, I met two women in their seventies who both happened to have worked in engineering, long before there were well-funded efforts to recruit women to STEM fields. They never had representation, but still succeeded in their careers. Representation, they felt, was irrelevant to success.

The second group strongly advocates for representation, saying that because God created diversity, we should be able to see it reflected in church, media, government, and so on. They may argue that lack of representation is racist and further proves systemic racism and believe representation and diversity should be a primary concern for all parts of society.

The third group is open but cautious. They believe some representation may be helpful, but also question how far to extend it. They may question whether every group needs to be represented in all circumstances. They tend to be concerned that insisting on representation for women or racial minorities might offer a pretext for activists with "identities" rooted in sinful behavior (such as LGBTQ+).

I've personally moved from being a strong advocate of representation to being "open but cautious." Some research indicates that minority children may have a more positive identity and perform better in school when they have teachers of the same race.[10] In a *Psychology Today* article titled "Why Representation Matters and Why It's Still Not Enough," author Kevin Nadal, PhD, states, "Representation can serve as opportunities for minoritized people to find community support and validation."[11] While I appreciate the work being done to argue for the best opportunities for children, we must remember that correlation does not necessarily equal causation. Are black students with black teachers doing better because the teachers are black, or because the teachers happen to be attentive and kind? I can see a case to be made that representation in places of leadership and media could help minority children dream about what's possible and increase their self-esteem. I can see the practical benefits of a child like Jenny having positive role models who share the same ethnicity or culture. I support representation for minority children adopted into white families *as long as the same provision is also made for white children adopted into minority families.*

I also have concerns about an underlying assumption that the lack of minority representation means systemic racism is at work. While that *might* be the case in some circumstances, it also *might not* be. Claims of this kind need to be researched and proven, not simply assumed. Additionally, advocacy for representation must not be allowed to undermine the reality of the universal human experience. All children long to be loved and to have a mother and father who love each other within a committed, stable marriage. Children of any ethnicity or culture need people of strong character and, ideally, Christian commitment in their lives. If we overemphasize the need for representation, we may be making ethnicity more important than character. This is a huge mistake. Godly parents and role models of any ethnicity can bridge cultural barriers, provide a stable and safe environment, love their children, and help them understand their creation and salvation identities. Healthy connections shouldn't be diminished simply because the people involved "don't match."

FINDING THE BALANCE

The gospel supernaturally unites people from across cultures and ethnicities, but it doesn't erase our cultural differences or language barriers. While the gospel confronts ethnic prejudices, the reality of human sin means ethnic prejudices still exist in the world. Interethnic families are learning daily how to live in this tension. Some have tried to respond by living the principles of colorblindness or taking up the mantle of antiracism. But the gospel offers a better way.

Rather than being "blind" to color and culture, the gospel frees us to see the world in full color. We can enjoy the very real differences of hair texture, language, and culture. Acknowledging our physical differences simply acknowledges how God has uniquely created each of us in His providence (Psalm 139:13-16). We can enjoy and celebrate the beauty of multiethnic families and the way they model the unity and diversity of the church. We don't ignore our providential differences, but we don't make them essential, either. Every Christian parent—whether raising their biological, monoethnic, or biracial child or navigating an interethnic adoption—is tasked with helping their child understand their three key identities in the proper order: creation identity, salvation identity, and secondary identities stemming from matters of providence. The way families implement this may vary, but the foundation remains the same. This framework can help provide relief for those biracial and adopted children who often feel the pressure to pick a side, such as which culture or ethnicity to identify with. No child should feel like they need to choose a side. Biblically speaking, there is only one side: human.

The risks and challenges of interracial adoption are real. Amazing, biblically grounded adoptive parents may face an adoptive child coming home from college and telling them that they are a racist. That one time Mom disliked his haircut: racist. Driving him to school or helping him with homework: racist. Disapproved of his music or his friend group: racist. Some parents live with the fear that this will unfold in their home in the future. Some are already experiencing it.

As I was writing this chapter, I encountered a young woman named Hope. She is the mother of a two-year-old biracial son, and she is also a very new Christian. Her son's father, who is black, sadly chose not to participate in their son's life, leaving her to raise him in a very white home with her very white parents in a very white town. Hope struggles to navigate conversations with others about her son's ethnicity. She faces the questions and challenges of whether she is "doing enough" to teach him about the other half of his culture and heritage. Like many parents, she has worried that as a white mother, she won't be able to adequately love and care for him.

Thankfully, a woman at Hope's church helped interrupt these insecurities, explaining that God has providentially entrusted Hope with her son. She encouraged her to raise him based on the Word of God and his identity in Christ, not the mandates of a confused and overly race-saturated culture.

Christian parents need to remember that God has entrusted them with each of their children as well. They won't have every answer to every situation they will face while raising their children, but they have the foundation. Hope knows she deeply loves her son and that she can trust God to lead them both on this journey. If you are a parent, so can you. Your child's primary identity is not in ethnicity, but in being fearfully and wonderfully made by the Creator—and God willing, your child will grow to become a faithful follower of Jesus. That is more than enough to help them weather whatever lies ahead.

REFLECTION QUESTIONS

1. What are the three points within the Christian worldview that support interethnic and intercultural marriage?

2. Look back on a time when you saw the representation of someone "like you" (in terms of race, culture, religion, class, ability, life circumstances, and so forth) in a movie, TV show, or another form of media. What impact, if any, did this have on you? What impact (positive or negative) has increasingly diverse representation in the media had on our culture in general?

3. What are the benefits of having diverse representation? To what extent do you believe this should be a priority? When do you think Christians should be cautious of diverse representation?

4. What is the difference between creation identity and salvation identity? How do these concepts provide an alternative for how the world presents issues of identity, especially when it comes to ethnicity?

5. How can you celebrate the way God has made you while also celebrating the different ways He has made others? Are there any changes you need to make in your language, standards, or behavior to better appreciate the vast beauty of the people He created?

CHAPTER 11

HOW DO WE TALK ABOUT RACE?

Krista Bontrager and Monique Duson

●●

(Monique) have always loved discussing race. Because of this, I thought talking to Krista about it would be easy. I just needed to explain privilege, white supremacy, and racial disparities to her. Easy enough! In reality, our conversations turned out to be some of the hardest I've ever had on any topic. While I couldn't see the benefits at the time, today I'm amazed by what God did through those conversations and our friendship.

STARTING THE CONVERSATION

Krista was mad! I mean, really mad! She was yelling and crying as we sat in the car, parked in our driveway.

"So no matter what I do, I am just always going to be a racist to you?" she was asking. "That's what you think of me? No matter what I do or don't do?"

I mean, she wasn't wrong; I did think she was a racist. Not the nasty, talk-bad-to-you-in-your-face kind of racist, but the other kind: the polite racist. The kind who blindly benefits from white systems, attends all-white churches with their all-white friends, and doesn't understand justice beyond praying, "God, please help them, and thanks that I'm not like them." I thought Krista was a racist who just didn't know it. I tried explaining that many times, and now she was upset.

The next day I told a black friend about Krista's reaction. Before I could finish, she responded "Girl, those are white tears!" She meant they are the tears white people cry to get out of conversations about race and racism, so they won't be perceived as racists. I didn't think Krista was using "white tears," and I had begun to doubt the things my friends and I all thought were true about white people. I said as much. My friend wasn't convinced. I went home, thinking about what she'd said: "Those are just white tears." I couldn't explain why that left me uneasy, but something felt different this time.

Conversations about race often rely on a prefabricated structure—a tangle of long and winding paths, dead ends that force you to find another route, and well-placed landmines that explode, blasting unexpecting travelers clear out of the conversation. Books like *Me and White Supremacy* and *How to Fight Racism* offer maps through the labyrinth antiracists created in the first place:[1]

> Start here: Understand the definition of racism and that all white people participate in racism.
>
> (If you're white) Turn right: Acknowledge your participation in complicit racism.
>
> (If you're black) Turn left: Acknowledge your systematized oppression.
>
> Go straight: Commit to the work of antiracism.
>
> (If you're white) Turn right: Lament and repent of your racism and white privilege.
>
> (If you're black) Turn left: Speak truth to power.

You get my point. Antiracists created a labyrinth, and only they can offer you the directions out of it.

So many people have been injured in this process. Our goal in starting the Center for Biblical Unity was to create a place where injured travelers of all ethnicities can find a safe space to discuss race, justice, and unity according to the rules of Scripture. The cultural narrative says minorities need respite from white people and assumes that white-dominated spaces are unsafe for blacks and other minorities. This isn't our position. People, regardless of ethnicity, are confused and hurting. And everyone needs a place to discuss and to heal.

IDENTITY IN CHRIST BEFORE ETHNIC IDENTITY

It took us a lot of time, conversation, and Bible study to realize that our primary identity is "children of God" and that we are, in fact, sisters. Gradually, we began shaking off the legalism of the "social justice pharisees"—those who dictate which actions must be taken and which books must be read for us to be seen as "good" people, doing justice rightly. We started walking in more freedom and joy with one another, rather than feeling emotionally exhausted all the time. We discovered that Christianity offers a better hope for unity than any cultural model ever could. And I began applying my mother's lessons about fighting for my biological family to fighting for my family in Christ.

One day, Krista and I found ourselves walking together and, surprisingly, not arguing. Instead, we brainstormed a list of our previous mistakes, calling them "barriers to racial unity." As we walked, Krista typed them into her phone. We identified several reasons why talking about race feels impossible for so many people:

- Nobody wants to be wrong. Everyone wants to be validated and heard, but very few engage in generous listening.

- Our defenses are up. Rather than have our feelings hurt by the other person, we seek to protect our heart and ideas, verbally "striking first," often lambasting the person in front of us.

- We have race conversations almost exclusively with people who think like us, creating an echo chamber in which we never hear any other perspectives. Social media often reinforces this.

- We assume that members of the "other" group won't care about our thoughts anyway, so we prefer not to take the risk of having the conversation.

- We make assumptions about who people are and what they believe based on skin color, instead of getting to know people as unique, fearfully and wonderfully made individuals.

- Racial reconciliation discussions have no clearly defined end goal, so we feel like we're on a never-ending hamster wheel of shame and frustration.

- We find it easier to engage in name-calling (like "racist," "race-baiter," "privileged") than to invest in actual relationships with people from another ethnicity or culture.

- We often fail to define terms clearly, and many ideas surrounding the discussion rest on definitions that are not based in biblical truth.

- We are too often unwilling to allow for mistakes, paralyzed by the fear of making mistakes, or unwilling to admit when we have made a mistake.

- We bring the pain of past hurtful conversations into our present conversations and assume that the person in front of us will interact with us the same way the last person did.

Despite the culture's demands and our past mistakes, Krista and I feel hopeful. Racial conversations don't have to be impossible. Scripture offers God's wisdom about how we can think, talk, and live together as Christian family. From it, we have drawn nine principles for healthy interactions with others about race.

Principle 1: Stay Present, Even When It's Hard

I (Monique) believe that one of the most effective skills for productive conversations is being present—staying alert to what the other person is saying now, not anticipating what we think they're going to say or jumping ahead to our next point. Being present also means choosing not to bring old conflicts with other people into the situation. We leave our assumptions at the door, and we tune in instead of tuning out. Despite frustrations that can arise, we deem the conversation and the other person as being worth the effort.

Emotional self-protection helps us feel safe and shields us from the pain of rejection in hard conversations, yet those same "protections" can become barriers to participating with each other in helpful ways. Knee-jerk responses, eye rolls, flaring tempers, annoyance, and impatience rarely, if ever, benefit the conversation. (I'm speaking as someone who knows this firsthand.) Although these are very human responses, they indicate a failure or refusal to be present and gracious with the other person. If we want to have helpful conversations about race, justice, and unity, we must do so from the present. Remember, the person in front of you bears the image of God and might also be your brother or sister in the Lord.

Principle 2: Be Honest, but with Grace

Being present requires being honest. Honesty in conversations about race is important but tricky. I (Monique) was raised to be honest—and even blunt! But not every family is like mine. At first, Krista struggled with how candidly and confidently I spoke about race and racism. She didn't want me to lie, yet the way I communicated was a struggle for her. I began to recognize that if I wanted her to understand my perspective, I needed to pay attention to how I communicated. And Krista also had to understand that honesty sometimes feels ugly and hard, even when our manner is gentle. But a difficult truth is better than a pretty lie.

Despite what racial reconciliation advocates and antiracists would have you believe, being honest doesn't mean your experience gives you special access to objective truth. Nor does it mean that the feelings attached to your experience prove that your perception of events is accurate, or that everyone in your group shares your experience. Sometimes feelings lie and memories cheat us. Honesty does not give you a license to unabashedly bulldoze others in conversation and should never be used as a weapon. Scripture tells us to be slow to speak, quick to listen, not easily angered, kind, and gracious with our words (Exodus 20:16; Colossians 3:9-10). Being both honest and gracious can help you open relational doors instead of close them, discover how ethnic partiality may have uniquely impacted the person you're talking to, or uncover reasons why the other person has been hesitant to engage in these conversations.

Be up-front about your fears, share specific experiences when relevant, and acknowledge your frustration when it arises, while also giving others room to explain themselves or correct themselves. Be willing to ask for clarity about someone's words or intent. If necessary, you can also ask for a time-out and commit to returning to the conversation later. Keep in mind that for Christians, listening is a two-way street of mutual respect and care. You may find it helpful to use phrases like:

"I'm afraid that in this conversation you're going to say/ think_____."

"I'd like to share how my experiences shape my perspective on this issue. Would you be open to hearing about that?"

"I noticed when you said _____, I started feeling frustrated because _____."

Principle 3: Integrate "Family" Language into Conversations

In my first video questioning some of the tenets of the racial reconciliation model, I (Monique) referred to white people as my brothers and sisters—as family—for the first time. The first time, that is, as a heartfelt statement, not a platitude. A year later, nearly to the day, I addressed a crowd of nearly two thousand people on the topic of race, starting with the words "Heeeeey, family!" You could feel the tension break. I believe those words helped put us all on the same level. I didn't brush over hard things in my presentation, but I did commit to facing hard topics with my audience as family.

Our culture is constantly slapping labels on people, but as Christians, we don't have to cooperate with this practice. In fact, Scripture calls us to a different way. In Christ, we are to no longer regard one another from a worldly point of view. God describes us as adopted (Ephesians 1:4-5), brothers and sisters (Hebrews 10:19), heirs with Christ (Romans 8:16-17), saved (Ephesians 2:8-9), and forgiven (Ephesians 4:31-32; Colossians 3:12-13). As members of God's household, our language about ourselves and each other should reflect God's views of us. Our words need to reflect that new reality.

Brothers and sisters from different ethnicities or cultural backgrounds are not enemies to be conquered or demeaned. They are family to be cherished. Because of this, Krista and I often use titles like *brother*, *sister*, and *cousin* for other Christians during our livestreams. We often use *uncle* or *aunty* to address the older men and women who have helped us grow in spiritual and biblical maturity (1 Timothy 5:1-2). These titles are a constant reminder that we belong to one another in God's family.

Principle 4: Lead with Curiosity Instead of Reactivity

Curiosity is an antidote to reactivity. I (Krista) have noticed that when my feelings are hurt, it's easy to react quickly with anger or frustration. But being patient, kind, and self-controlled demonstrates the Holy Spirit living within us (Galatians 5:22-23). Reacting in hasty anger is a "work of the flesh" (Galatians 5:19-21). Chronic and habitual rage without repentance is a sign of an unbeliever.

Curiosity can help reveal assumptions that are often at the root of conflicts. If you think a conversation may become tense, step back and take note of your own assumptions and emotions first. Check in with yourself. Are you harboring any resentments from your last conversation with that person—or someone else who may have sounded like them? (This was a major problem for me. I had experienced significant trauma over race issues with a former colleague. I tended to drag all those emotions into early conversations with Monique.) Are you feeling anxious, afraid, or tense as you begin the conversation? Do you need to forgive or ask for forgiveness?

Then, be curious about the other person's beliefs and experiences. Don't assume you know his or her heart simply because of something previously said or a post you saw on social media. Your assumptions may be right...or wrong. It's important not to write off a person or the validity of their points just because you "knew they would say that."

Check in with the other person later too. Ask: "What thoughts have you had about this since we last spoke?" Sometimes opinions change between conversations. Sometimes they don't. Find out where the other person stands now and engage anew.

Curiosity is vital for productive conversations. Not only will it help you understand opposing views, but it also shows you are seeking to understand and not just to be right. Asking thoughtful questions can help dissipate initial emotions and help us extend the benefit of the doubt to others. You can also show respect by letting others ask you questions or checking to see if they would like you to clarify anything you've said. Keep your goals in mind and reaffirm your commitment to the relationship. You may find some of the following questions and statements helpful:

- I'd really like to understand your perspective on this.

- Can you describe three feelings you are experiencing at this moment?

- Can you help me understand your position better?

- What do you mean by that?

- What is a biblical definition for that term or idea? (That one frequently made Monique angry in the moment, but as her biblical knowledge grew, the question became more effective.)

- What are some resources that might help me understand your position better?

Principle 5: Investigate Claims of Racism, and Examine the Evidence Before Forming a Conclusion

Viral videos of racist events can quickly stir our emotions. But before pressing the share button on social media, make sure to step back and ask some deeper questions. Jumping to conclusions and letting emotions run amok is neither helpful nor biblical. Our culture has programmed us to believe any uncomfortable interaction between a white person and a member of an ethnic minority is likely the result of racism. We need to resist this temptation and instead take time to gather more information and respond appropriately.

The Bible requires more than just one witness's story before reaching judgments about someone's guilt (Deuteronomy 17:6; Matthew 18:16; 1 Timothy 5:19). One person's "lived experience," subjective perceptions about racism, or generalizing about an entire group of people based on the actions of one (or even a few) is not enough to meet the biblical criteria for a just pronunciation of guilt. Look into corroborating evidence, including the testimony of eye-witnesses, text messages, police reports, or other forms of evidence that come from objective, primary sources, not hearsay. When an accusation of racism is made, leaders can respond best by remaining calm and investigating the charge carefully. Racism is a serious charge, and proper evidence needs to be gathered.

Just yesterday, an older white man pulled up beside me (Monique) at a stoplight and started yelling at me. I had been minding my own business, blasting gospel music in the car. I sat there, trying to resist (but failing) jumping to the conclusion "He's a racist."

Suddenly, he blurted, "Go back to California!"

I laughed so hard and said, "Oh! You're not a racist! You're a state-ist!"

He must have noticed my license plate. Maybe that man felt like Arizona had enough Californians already, or that all Californians are bad drivers. Not every difficult situation involving people from different races is motivated by racism. Actions might be motivated by stateism, fashionism, ageism, tattooism, or any other prejudice we could slap an "ism" on.

After one of our public events, Krista and I spoke with a biracial high school student who asked us how to confront a teacher she believed was racist. When we asked for more information, she struggled to give us specific evidence of racism. Still, some of the teacher's actions had hurt her feelings. She was stunned when I asked if she had considered any other possible reasons for her teacher's actions. As we explored several of them together, this young lady realized she didn't have enough data to pinpoint her teacher's motive. It was as if five hundred pounds of anger lifted off her shoulders. She was no longer pigeonholed into believing the worst about her teacher and could begin seeing her as a fellow human being. She had the freedom to investigate before making judgments.

A fair exploration of possibilities doesn't deny the reality of racism. Racism is real. People are sinners. Race-based bias happens. It's one of the possibilities. But serious charges should not be levied over every hurt feeling or negative interaction between members of different races. Be a detective, dive into the data, and inspect the evidence. If racism is really happening, then address it responsibly and biblically. And if not, do whatever that situation calls for responsibly and biblically as well.

Principle 6: Do Your Own Homework, and Process What You're Learning with Others

Having a thoughtful dialogue partner when you're on the growing edge of learning something new can be very helpful. At the same time, we must be careful not to become overdependent on our dialogue partners. Early in our friendship, I (Krista) asked Monique questions almost nonstop. I was in a growing season, trying to understand her perspective and devouring a lot of content.

One day, she told me, "Do your own research. Girl, I'm not Google." Monique wanted me to understand that being black doesn't make her an expert in all things black or enable her to speak for all black people. And think about it: Even experts can get tired of constantly talking about their area of expertise at dinner parties and church events. Imagine being a doctor and having every person you run into ask for free medical advice. That would get old.

Interpersonal conversations can be helpful, and there should be space to get help processing what you're learning. Still, we must also take responsibility to dig deeper into a subject by reading books or listening to podcasts from reputable sources. Don't turn your friends into your own personal encyclopedia. And remember that when it comes to conversations about race, not every member of a particular ethnic group has the same point of view, expertise, or interest in the discussion. Strike a balance between doing your own research and reaching out for help. Be thoughtful, be respectful, and reach out when appropriate.

Principle 7: Be Patient with the Process

Thoughtful dialogue and healthy growth require patience with yourself, with others, and with God. You don't have to have an answer to every question. If you don't know something, you can come back to that topic in a future conversation. Accept that you will likely get some things wrong or say something insensitive (even when you're trying not to). When this happens, own it and ask for forgiveness if you've sinned. Be patient with the other person too. He or she is likely experiencing some of the same emotions as you, so extend grace and be willing to take a break if one of you needs to calm down or think things over before returning to the conversation.

Also, be patient with the Lord and what He may be doing with both of you. Don't put yourself or others on a timeline. Trust God to bring them along. Krista spent a long time asking me (Monique) strategic questions, without clear progress. During this process, the Lord orchestrated events in my life that eroded my trust in the racial reconciliation model and brought me toward biblical unity. Patience can be hard, but it is evidence of our life in Christ (Galatians 5:22; 1 Corinthians 13:4).

Principle 8: Be Generous in Grace and Forgiveness for Mistakes

Human beings are deeply flawed, and we all make mistakes. Sometimes we sin against each other. And sometimes we hold on to resentment toward others for the sins we've also committed. Understand that in conversations of race, we will all make mistakes and missteps at some point. Whether those things are intentional or not, we need to repent and make things right with those we have hurt. Krista has a saying: "In order for two sinners to walk in peace, there must be both generous repentance and generous forgiveness" (based on Matthew 18).

When you make a mistake, acknowledge what has happened and repent quickly. In our culture, asking for forgiveness can be seen as a weakness. But for Christians, admitting when we are wrong and taking responsibility for our mistakes are acts of obedience to Christ. Genuine repentance is the mark of a humble heart being transformed by the Holy Spirit.

Christ calls us not only to seek forgiveness, but to extend it (Ephesians 4:32). When someone is trying to repair the relationship, provide forgiveness quickly. Even when their apology is awkward and feels incomplete, don't withhold forgiveness and harbor pride in your heart. Whatever offenses others have committed against us, we have committed far worse against God. Forgiveness is an acknowledgment of our need for God's generosity and forgiveness toward us (Matthew 18:15-25).

In October 2019, off-duty Dallas police officer Amber Guyger shot to death a black man named Botham Jean in his apartment. Guyger told officials she entered the wrong apartment, thinking it was her own, and shot Jean because she believed he was an intruder in her home. The jury found her guilty of murder.[2] During Guyger's sentencing, the victim's brother, Brandt Jean, addressed her from the witness stand. "I forgive you," he said, and encouraged her to also accept Christ's salvation and forgiveness. With the judge's permission, Brandt hugged Guyger, a moment that later went viral on social media. It became the hug seen around the world. Many saw this as a tangible public display of the power of the gospel and the beauty of forgiveness.

But some racial reconciliation advocates disagreed. Jemar Tisby wrote an opinion piece for the *Washington Post* expressing concern that Brandt's personal act of forgiveness would be seen as some kind of symbolic act of forgiveness extended to all white people for historic injustices against black people. He argued that a "society built around white superiority is also built around white innocence—an assumption of the intrinsic moral virtue of all white people and the purity of their intentions regardless of impact. White innocence assumes black forgiveness."[3]

According to Tisby, expecting all black people to extend forgiveness as quickly as Brandt Jean did demonstrates a poor understanding of black people and "black pain." Tisby's article reflects a hesitancy among some in the black community to be generous in forgiveness toward others, especially when an offense involves white people. Some black people are instructed not to offer "black forgiveness" too quickly.

The main problem isn't forgiving too quickly. The main problem is sinful hearts. Both unforgiveness and unrepentance are contrary to biblical teachings. Personally, I (Krista) believe that what made that hug between Brandt Jean and Amber Guyger so powerful was not that black forgiveness was expected or that white innocence was presumed. I think the moment moved so many people because the forgiveness was so undeserved. Public displays of generous grace are rare. Watching them takes your breath away.

Biblical unity requires a balance of repentance and forgiveness. Repentance without forgiveness leads to despair. Holding on to resentment toward repentant wrongdoers or dragging the burdens of the past into the present can cause endless damage. And forgiveness without repentance can lead to abuse. If someone in your life is constantly demeaning you or engaging in repeated, unrepentant behavior toward you because of your ethnicity, get some emotionally and biblically mature brothers and sisters to help you arbitrate the issue and provide support. Forgiveness is not a shield for continued sin or abuse.

Practicing forgiveness can be as difficult, if not more, than repentance. Living out the principles of Ephesians 4:31-32 is hard when we believe holding on to bitterness and anger is justified. But forgiveness isn't just a command to obey; it's also for our good. God knows that unforgiveness hurts us just as much as—or even more than—it hurts the person we are angry with. Bitterness, rage, and slander are also sins against God that hinder our relationship with Him. And if God, being so generous to extend forgiveness to us through Jesus, requires us to forgive one another, how can we refuse? Following Christ means obeying His commands, even when it means forgiving our enemies (Luke 6:27-28).

God's household rules, including repentance and forgiveness, exist for the benefit of others, ourselves, and our relationship with Him. True unity can't be achieved without true forgiveness.

Principle 9: Don't Make Every Conversation about Race

About six months after starting CFBU, Krista and I (Monique) found our friendship suffering. We didn't do fun things anymore. We didn't just sit and talk about random things; everything had become about race. One day she sat down next to me and said, "I miss you." Race had taken up so much of our conversations and mental space that a small chasm had formed between us. Early on, we had committed to not allow conversations of race to destroy our friendship. While we weren't at risk of losing our friendship, we were losing the beauty and laughter that made our friendship enjoyable and unique.

Culture has trained us to think we must constantly talk about race if we want to be kind, compassionate, and relevant. I disagree. We must stop believing the lie that we are participating in racism whenever we are not talking or posting about it. Centralizing race in our friendships and national conversations may do more harm than good. Conversations on race and racism are vital, yet they can become all-encompassing. That's not healthy or helpful. The Scriptures don't make race or ethnicity a primary focal point, and I strongly caution against allowing race to become the focal point of your friendships.

THE BOTTOM LINE

We both believe these nine principles provide a healthier guide for navigating the labyrinth of modern racial conversations more biblically and wisely. When we participate with one another from a place of mutual respect and care, we can hold difficult conversations without damaging other people. When we make our commitment to each other as brothers and sisters in Christ the starting point of conversations within the church, we can overcome common barriers to racial unity. God's grace and forgiveness provides our hope as Christians. Grace and forgiveness for each other provides hope for walking out our unity in Christ.

Our culture's racial reconciliation and antiracism frameworks can't deliver unity, inside or outside the church, because they rely on deficient and unbiblical ideas for their vision to be achieved. We cannot meet culture on its own terms and expect it to result in unity. The path to unity involves Christians participating with one another as

Christ commands. It also involves bringing the gospel to those who are outside the family so they can be invited into biblical unity as well.

God's plan for unity—ethnic or otherwise—is accomplished through the blood of Christ. Unity is lived out first within His family, the church. Scripture does not lay out a plan for how non-Christians can walk in unity or for how Christians can walk in unity with non-Christians.

As Christians are discipled to obey all Jesus's commands (Matthew 28:19-20), we proclaim the gospel, plant more churches, disciple new believers, and live counterculturally before the world. In doing so, we show non-Christians that there is a better hope for ethnic unity than we can achieve by human efforts alone. Treating cultural enemies with love, patience, and humility is not natural to sinful human beings. We need Christ to make us new.

The beauty of Christianity, in contrast to secular worldviews, is that it offers a better hope for healing, justice, and unity. Where culture encourages contention and resentment, the gospel brings peace. The world says that reconciliation comes through favoritism and unity comes through striving. Christianity says reconciliation comes through Christ, not our works, and that striving ceases at the foot of the cross. This is good news for everyone, of every ethnicity and skin tone! It is Jesus who restores all things and makes us one family. He is the foundation of our unity.

God's truth is that those who trust in Christ are truly brothers and sisters, no matter how much melanin we have! And all of us, regardless of skin tone, share the same responsibilities to walk in unity… together. We all must walk in humility, kindness, and gentleness. We all must extend generous forgiveness. That's the way of Christ. And the world can't help but notice it.

REFLECTION QUESTIONS

1. Which of the reasons why it's hard to talk about race (outlined on pages 210-211) resonates with you the most? In your own life, where have you faced the most challenges when it comes to discussing this sensitive subject?

2. What does it look like to practice honesty with grace? Which half of that equation is the most challenging for you?

3. How can Monique's advice to "face [your] audience as a family" positively influence the perspective you take when addressing others (especially those who are different from you)?

4. How can you balance the principle of "leading with curiosity" with "doing your own homework"? Do these two principles seem mutually exclusive to you? How would you apply them in different circumstances?

5. Why is it important to investigate claims and evidence of racism for yourself before drawing a conclusion? How does this dovetail with the imperative to "judge rightly" that was discussed in chapter 4?

NOTES

INTRODUCTION: FINDING FRIENDSHIP

1. For more information about our center, see www.centerforbiblicalunity.com.

CHAPTER 1: HOW DID WE BECOME SO DIVIDED?

1. The universal understanding in the black community at that time was that Rodney King was beaten by "four white officers"; this is also how it was reported, largely, by the mainstream media at the time. It is not lost on me that Theodore Briseno is one-quarter Hispanic, but at the time, that was an incidental detail that went largely overlooked. "LAPD Officers Beat Rodney King on Camera," History, March 3, 1991, https://www.history.com/this-day-in-history/police-brutality-caught-on-video.

2. Brenda E. Stevenson, "Latasha Harlins, Soon Ja Du, and Joyce Karlin: A Case Study of Multicultural Female Violence and Justice on the Urban Frontier," *The Journal of African American History* 89, no. 2 (Spring 2004): 152–76, https://doi.org/10.2307/4134098.

3. Ibid., 165.

4. Adam Gurowski, *The History of Slavery* (Madison & Adams Press, 2019), 56–59.

5. WGBH, "Africans in America: From Indentured Servitude to Racial Slavery," PBS.org, 2019, https://www.pbs.org/wgbh/aia/part1/1narr3_txt.html.

6. Louis T. Talbot, "Studies in Genesis–13," Talbot Publications (2017), 4, https://digitalcommons.biola.edu/talbot-pub/58.

7. Ibid., 5.

8. Robert P. Jones, *White Too Long: The Legacy of White Supremacy in American Christianity* (New York: Simon & Schuster, 2021), 17.

9. See http://www.history.com/news/the-father-of-modern-gynecology-performed-shocking-experiments-on-slaves.

10. "'11 A.M. Sunday Is Our Most Segregated Hour'; In the Light of the Racial Crisis, a Christian Leader Assays 'the Structure and Spirit' of the Nation's Churches, and Asks Some Probing Questions," *New York Times*, August 2, 1964, https://www.nytimes.com/1964/08/02/archives/11-a-m-sunday-is-our-most-segregated-hour-in-the-light-of-the.html.

11. Curtis J. Evans, "White Evangelical Protestant Responses to the Civil Rights Movement," *Harvard Theological Review* 102, no. 2 (April 2009): 245-73, https://doi.org/10.1017/s0017816009000765.

12. Ibid.

13. Adelle Banks, "Study: Black Christians See Limits to Multiracial Churches," *Christianity Today*, April 29, 2021, https://www.christianitytoday.com/news/2021/april/racial-division-church-multi racial-diverse-study.html.

14. Francis Newton Thorpe, *The History of North America: The Colonization of the South*, by P. J. Hamilton (New York, NY: Nabu Press: 2010 [1904]), 113.

15. "'An Act Declaring That Baptisme of Slaves Doth Not Exempt Them from Bondage' (1667)," Encyclopedia Virginia, https://encyclopediavirginia.org/entries/an-act-declaring-that-baptisme -of-slaves-doth-not-exempt-them-from-bondage-1667.

16. Richard I. McKinney, "The Black Church: Its Development and Present Impact," *Harvard Theological Review* 64, no. 4 (October 1971): 452-81, http://www.jstor.org/stable/1509098.

17. James H. Cone, *God of the Oppressed* (Maryknoll, NY: Orbis Books, 1997), 34-35, Kindle edition.

18. James H. Cone, *Black Theology and Black Power* (Maryknoll, NY: Orbis Books, 2018), 41.

19. "Second, the White Church fails in its service. Diakonia, as defined by Cone, consists in the Church 'joining Christ in his work of liberation.' Cone leans heavily here on his understanding of atonement. Christ as victorious over evil in His death on the cross is significant as an act of liberation for those who suffer from the evil of oppression. If Jesus focuses His work on liberation, then the Church's necessary service must mirror Christ's in its act of liberating the oppressed from the old evil powers. The Church's contemporary context must assume that the central evil power at work is racism arising from white supremacy. Thus, the diakonia the Church must render to the world is service that attacks racism at its source and places the Church in solidarity with the oppressed black community. This service is made all the more important by the fact that, though Christ's defeat of evil is decisive, the war against evil continues to rage." Joseph W. Caldwell, "A Starting Point for Understanding James Cone: A Primer for White Readers," *Review & Expositor* 117, no. 1 (February 2020): 25-43, https://doi .org/10.1177/0034637320903046.

20. Henry Louis Gates Jr., *Black Church: This Is Our Story, This Is Our Song* (New York: Penguin Press, 2021), 97.

21. Langston Hughes, "The Negro Mother," in *The Negro Mother and Other Dramatic Recitations*, by Langston Hughes, illustrated by Prentiss Taylor (1931), Prentiss Taylor papers, 1885–1991. Archives of American Art, Smithsonian Institution.

22. "The 1619 Project," *New York Times Magazine*, August 14, 2019, https://www.nytimes.com/ interactive/2019/08/14/magazine/1619-america-slavery.html.

23. The Historian, "Black Slave Owners–10 Most Famous," Have Fun with History, December 27, 2022, https://www.havefunwithhistory.com/black-slave-owners/.

24. Mark Sherman, "Supreme Court to Hear Challenge to Affirmative Action in College Admissions," PBS NewsHour, January 24, 2022, https://www.pbs.org/newshour/education/ supreme-court-to-hear-challenge-to-race-in-college-admissions.

25. "God declares that the woman will have pain in childbirth. There will also be strife between

her and her husband. The unity and transparency between the man and woman has been broken. When the promised descendant of the woman comes, the original unity will be restored. There will no longer be Jew nor Gentile, slave nor free, male nor female (Gal. 3:28). In Christ, all these judgments will be reversed." "Genesis 3:16," *NIV Grace and Truth Study Bible* (Grand Rapids: Zondervan, 2021).

CHAPTER 2: HOW SHOULD CHRISTIANS THINK ABOUT RACIAL UNITY?

1. James H. Cone, *Black Theology and Black Power* (Maryknoll, NY: Orbis Books, 2018), 222, Kindle edition.

2. This definition is a combination of my own definition and Robin DiAngelo's definition, which is found in the *International Journal of Critical Pedagogy*, Vol. 3 (3), (2011), 54-70.

3. Ruth Frankenberg, *White Women, Race Matters: The Social Construction of Whiteness* (Minneapolis: University of Minnesota Press, 1993), iv.

4. https://nmaahc.si.edu/learn/talking-about-race/topics/whiteness.

5. For more on what it means to "do the work" of antiracism, see https://slate.com/podcasts/how-to/2024/04/how-to-do-the-work-of-racial-justice.

6. Patricia Bidol-Padva, *Developing New Perspectives on Race: An Innovative Multi-Media Social Studies Curriculum in Racism Awareness for the Secondary Level* (Detroit: New Perspectives on Race, 1972).

7. Ambalavaner Sivanandan, *Communities of Resistance* (New York: Verso Books, 1990), 99.

8. Darrell Bock, Derwin Gray, Chad Brennan, and Christina Barland Edmondson, "Reconciliation or Antiracism?," November 3, 2022, webinar by *Christianity Today* and Seminary Now, https://www.christianitytoday.com/ct/2022/october-web-only/reconciliation-or-antiracism.html. Emphasis added.

9. Ibid.

10. Ibid. Emphasis added.

11. "Robin DiAngelo, Ph.D.," LinkedIn profile, https://www.linkedin.com/in/robin-diangelo-phd, accessed July 1, 2023.

12. Robin DiAngelo, *White Fragility* (Boston: Beacon Press, 2018), 20. Emphasis added.

13. Beverly Daniel Tatum, "Defining Racism: Can We Talk?," in Maurianne Adams et al., eds., *Readings for Diversity and Social Justice*, 4th ed. (London: Routledge, 2018), 80. Emphasis added.

14. Ibram X. Kendi, *How to Be an Antiracist* (New York: One World, 2019), 20.

15. George A. Yancey, *Beyond Racial Gridlock: Embracing Mutual Responsibility* (Downers Grove, IL: Intervarsity Press, 2006), 26-27.

16. Barna Group, "White Christians Have Become Even Less Motivated to Address Racial Injustice," Barna.com, September 15, 2020, https://www.barna.com/research/american-christians-race-problem/.

17. *Why You Think the Way You Do* by Glenn Sunshine offers a wonderful survey of Christianity's unique contribution to human dignity (Zondervan, 2009).

18. This particular wording is from Article 1 of the Lausanne Covenant. However, the doctrine of God's providence can be found across Christian traditions, including the Westminster Confession of Faith, 5.1-5.4; Belgic Confession, article 13; and the 1689 Baptist Confession of Faith, chapter 5.

CHAPTER 3: WHAT DOES THE BIBLE HAVE TO SAY ABOUT RACIAL UNITY?

1. *Merriam-Webster Dictionary*, s.v. "race," accessed May 30, 2023, https://www.merriam-web ster.com/dictionary/race#usage-1.

2. Ibid.

3. "Race & Ethnicity," US Census Bureau, January 2017, https://www.cosb.us/home/ showpublisheddocument/5935/637356700118370000.

4. "Ethnicity," US Census Bureau, accessed July 7, 2023, https://www.census.gov/glossary/? term=Ethnicity.

5. Beverly M. Pratt, Lindsay Hixson, and Nicholas A. Jones, "Measuring Race and Ethnicity across the Decades: 1790–2010," US Census Bureau, https:// www.census.gov/data-tools/demo/race/ MREAD_1790_2010.html.

6. David R. Roediger, "Historical Foundations of Race," National Museum of African American History and Culture, Smithsonian Institute, https://nmaahc.si.edu/learn/talking-about-race/ topics/historical-foundations-race.

7. Immanuel Kant, "Of the Different Races of Human Beings (1775)" in *Anthropology, History, and Education* (Cambridge University Press, 2013), 82-97, https://doi.org/10.1017/ CBO9780511791925.007.

8. Georg Forster, *A Voyage Round the World*, vol. I, eds. Nicholas Thomas and Oliver Berghof (Honolulu: University of Hawaii Press, 2000), 221, as quoted by Sally Hatch Gray, "Kant's Race Theory, Forster's Counter, and the Metaphysics of Color," *The Eighteenth Century: Theory and Interpretation* 53, no. 4 (Winter 2012): 393, https://www.jstor.org/stable/23365038.

9. Ann Gibbons, "New Gene Variants Reveal the Evolution of Human Skin Color," *Science*, October 12, 2017, https://www.science.org/content/article/new-gene-variants-reveal-evolution -human-skin-color.

10. For an early summary of the human genome project findings, see Natalie Angier, "Do Races Differ? Not Really, Genes Show," *New York Times*, August 22, 2000, https://www.nytimes.com /2000/08/22/science/do-races-differ-not-really-genes-show.html.

11. For a Christian perspective on human origins, we recommend the book *Who Was Adam?: A Creation Model Approach to the Origin of Man* by Fazale Rana and Hugh Ross (Colorado Springs: NavPress, 2015).

12. "The Five Most Common Ashkenazi Genetic Diseases," National Goucher Foundation, https:// www.gaucherdisease.org/blog/5-common-ashkenazi-genetic-diseases/.

13. Usually, the clip that is shared on social media resembles this: For the New Christian Intellectual,

"'I Am a Racist'—Matthew Hall, Provost at Southern Seminary," YouTube, July 31, 2019, https://youtu.be/1IiKCYSevDU. The discussion in its entirety can be viewed here: Coffee and Cream, "13: Seminaries and Racial Reconciliation with Matthew Hall," YouTube, July 18, 2018, https://www.youtube.com/watch?v=dwI82hKUTgI.

14. Matthew J. Hall, "'For He Is Our Peace': The Centrality of the Gospel of Christ in Racial Reconciliation," Southern Equip, November 26, 2019. https://equip.sbts.edu/article/peace-centrality-gospel-christ-racial-reconciliation. Hall published a follow-up essay making many of the same points in 2021: Matthew J. Hall, "Why I'm Not Giving Up on Racial Reconciliation," Matthew J. Hall.net, June 24, 2021, https://www.matthewjhall.net/articles/why-im-not-giving-up-on-racial-reconciliation.

15. Dr. Martin Luther King Jr., "I Have a Dream," August 28, 1963, National Public Radio, https://www.npr.org/2010/01/18/122701268/i-have-a-dream-speech-in-its-entirety.

CHAPTER 4: WHAT IS RACISM?

1. Erica Eisen, "Specimen Days: Human Zoos at the 1904 World's Fair," *Lady Science*, February 14, 2019, https://thenewinquiry.com/blog/specimen-days-human-zoos-at-the-1904-worlds-fair.

2. Charles Darwin, *The Descent of Man*, illustrated (Independently published, 2017), 48, https://a.co/d/gl73tyl.

3. For example, on page 31, Darwin compares various "civilized" and "barbarous" "races" to "domesticated" and wild animals.

4. G. K. Chesterton, *Eugenics and Other Evils*, ed. Michael W. Perry (Seattle: Inkling Books, 2000).

5. "Racial Equity Tools Glossary," Racial Equity Tools, https://www.racialequitytools.org/glossary.

6. Ibid., "Individual Racism."

7. Ibid., "Interpersonal Racism."

8. Ibid., "Institutional Racism."

9. Ibid., "Structural Racism."

10. Ibid., "Systemic Racism."

11. Ibid., "Internalized Racism."

12. Epiphany Fellowship, "Overcoming the Stronghold of Racism—May 2nd, 2021," YouTube, May 2, 2021, approx. 47:00, https://www.youtube.com/ watch?v=6eOx_e9KNlg. Emphasis added.

13. Ibid. Emphasis added.

14. Patrick Kline, Evan Rose, and Christopher Walters, "Systemic Discrimination among Large U.S. Employers," University of Chicago, Becker Friedman Institute for Economics Working Paper No. 2021-94, August 3, 2021, https:// doi.org/10.2139/ssrn.3898669.

15. There are many studies to this effect, with varying ways of measuring the effectiveness of the Equal Opportunity Act. Here are just two examples: Marianne Bertrand and Sendhil Mullainathan, "Are Emily and Greg More Employable than Lakisha and Jamal? A Field Experiment on Labor Market Discrimination," *American Economic Review* 94, no. 4 (September 2004):

991-1013, https://doi.org/10.1257/0002828042002561; Jerry M. Newman, "Discrimination in Recruitment: An Empirical Analysis," *Industrial & Labor Relations Review* 32, no. 1 (October 1978): 15-23, https://doi.org/10.2307/2522415.

CHAPTER 5: HOW SHOULD WE THINK
ABOUT SYSTEMIC INJUSTICE?

1. Derwin Gray, "We Have to Raise the Bar on Racial Justice," *Relevant Magazine*, April 5, 2022, https://relevantmagazine.com/justice/derwin-gray-we-have-to-raise-the-bar-on-racial-justice. Emphasis added.

2. Frederick Douglass, *Frederick Douglass: Selected Speeches and Writings*, The Library of Black America, eds., Philip S. Foner and Yuval Taylor (Chicago: Chicago Review Press, 2000), 653, https://a.co/d/2NlAM8t.

3. Özlem Sensoy and Robin J. DiAngelo, *Is Everyone Really Equal?*, 2nd ed. (New York: Teachers College Press, 2017), 125.

4. Ibid.

5. This is a statement Tisby frequently makes. Here is just one example of it from a chapel message given at Wheaton College on October 30, 2019: WheatonCollege, "Jemar Tisby: Complicity in Racism (10/30/2019)," YouTube, November 15, 2019, 22:55, https://www.youtube.com/watch?v=TjdGvGQ6RgA.

6. Richard Delgado and Jean Stefancic, eds., *The Derrick Bell Reader* (New York: NYU Press, 2005), 85.

7. Jude 3 Project, "Change the Story | Lisa Fields," YouTube, August 30, 2019, 12:19, https://www.youtube.com/watch?v=uibBJVEMWnU.

8. Phillip Holmes, Jim Davis, and Justin Holcomb, "Individual Racism vs. Systemic Racism," TGC Podcast, October 29, 2020, https://www.thegospelcoalition.org/podcasts/as-in-heaven/individual-racism-systemic-racism.

9. Ibid.

10. Ibid.

11. The grandfather clauses exempted people whose grandfathers could vote (white people) from "restrictions" on voting. Everyone (white or black) had to take a literacy test or pay a poll tax *unless* their grandfather had been allowed to vote. Effectively, that disenfranchised most black people. It was a devious way of circumventing the Fourteenth and Fifteenth Amendments.

12. Richard Rothstein, "Public Housing: Government-Sponsored Segregation," *The American Prospect*, October 11, 2012, https://prospect.org/article/public-housing-government-sponsored-segregation.

13. "Housing Discrimination under the Fair Housing Act," US Department of Housing and Urban Development, https://www.hud.gov/program_offices/fair housing_equal_opp/fair_housing_act_overview.

14. Paula A. Braveman et al., "Systemic and Structural Racism: Definitions, Examples, Health Damages, and Approaches to Dismantling," *Health Affairs* 41, no. 2 (February 2022): 171-78, https://doi.org/10.1377/hlthaff.2021.01394.

15. Thomas Sowell, *Discrimination and Disparities* (New York: Basic Books, 2019), 88-89.

16. Racial Equity Tools, s.v. "Implicit Bias," racialequitytools.org, https://www.racialequitytools.org/glossary.

17. Saul Mcleod, "Carl Jung's Theory of Personality: Archetypes & Collective Unconscious," Simply Psychology (January 24, 2024), https://www.simplypsychology.org/carl-jung.html.

18. John Bell, "The Four 'I's' of Oppression," https://www.joliet86.org/assets/1/6/Four_Is_of_Oppression.pdf.

19. Richard Rothstein, *The Color of Law: A Forgotten History of How Our Government Segregated America* (New York: Liveright Publishing Corporation, 2017).

CHAPTER 6: SHOULD CHRISTIANS WORK TOWARD RACIAL RECONCILIATION?

1. Fellowship Church, "The Family Table—Albert Tate," Vimeo, June 14, 2020, https://vimeo.com/429033759.

2. Ibid.

3. Carolyn Carney, "4 Steps White People Can Take towards Racial Reconciliation," Intervarsity Multiethnic Ministries, https://mem.intervarsity.org/resources/4-steps-white-people-can-take-towards-racial-reconciliation.

4. Ibid.

5. "Racial Justice Glossary of Terms," Be the Bridge, https://bethebridge.com/racial-justice-glossary-of-terms.

6. "16 Bridge-Building Tips for White People," Be the Bridge, 2019, https://bethebridge.com/docs/16Tips.pdf.

7. Ibid.

8. Eric Mason, *Woke Church: An Urgent Call for Christians in America to Confront Racism and Injustice* (Chicago: Moody Publishers, 2018), 41.

9. Tony Evans, *Oneness Embraced: A Kingdom Race Theology for Reconciliation, Unity, and Justice* (Chicago: Moody Publishers, 2022), 371.

CHAPTER 7: HOW DO WE WALK IN UNITY?

1. Neil Smelser, "Sources of Unity and Disunity in Sociology," *The American Sociologist* 46, no. 3 (September 2015): 303-12, https://doi.org/10.1007/s12108-015-9260-2.

2. James Cone, *God of the Oppressed* (Maryknoll, New York: Orbis Books, 1997), 22.

3. Ibid, 222.

4. Ibid.

5. See https://youtu.be/SxeEhuT4Cao?si=lNi6SXMC15iuYA5a.

CHAPTER 8: SHOULD WE REPENT FOR THE SINS OF OUR ANCESTORS?

1. Isabella Rosario, "The Unlikely Story Behind Japanese Americans' Campaign for Reparations," NPR Code Switch, March 24, 2020, https://www.npr.org/sections/codeswitch/2020/03/24/820181127/the-unlikely-story-behind-japanese-americans-campaign-for-reparations.

2. Se Eun Gong, "U.S. Allies South Korea and Japan Move Closer to Resolve Forced Labor Feud," NPR, March 6, 2023, https://www.npr.org/2023/03/06/1161250054/u-s-allies-south-korea-and-japan-move-closer-to-resolve-forced-labor-feud.

3. Washington Journal, "William Darity on Reparations and Campaign 2020," C-SPAN, March 21, 2019, https://www.c-span.org/video/?458905-4/william- darity-reparations-campaign -2020&event=458905&playEvent.

4. Thabiti Anyabwile, "Reparations Are Biblical," The Gospel Coalition, October 10, 2019, https://www.thegospelcoalition.org/blogs/thabiti-anyabwile/reparations-are-biblical.

5. Epiphany Fellowship, "CANCEL CULTURE | A Biblical Case for Reparations| Dr. Eric Mason," YouTube, August 26, 2020, https://www.youtube.com/watch?v=7jwf0o9nYWA.

6. Tony Evans, *Oneness Embraced: A Kingdom Race Theology for Reconciliation, Unity, and Justice* (Chicago: Moody Publishers, 2022), 247.

7. Tim Keller, "Racism and Corporate Evil: A White Guy's Perspective," Desiring God, March 28, 2012, https://www.desiringgod.org/messages/racism-and-corporate-evil.

8. Ibid.

CHAPTER 9: SHOULD ALL CHURCHES BE MULTIETHNIC?

1. "'11 A.M. Sunday Is Our Most Segregated Hour'; In the Light of the Racial Crisis, a Christian Leader Assays 'the Structure and Spirit' of the Nation's Churches, and Asks Some Probing Questions," *New York Times*, August 2, 1964, https://www.nytimes.com/1964/08/02/archives/11-a-m-sunday-is-our-most-segregated-hour-in-the-light-of-the.html.

2. "Richard Allen: First Elected and Consecrated Bishop in the AME Church," AME Social Action Commission, https://ame-sac.org/ames-in-history/richard-allen.

3. "The Great Walkout…," The African Episcopal Church of St. Thomas, http://www.aecst.org/walkout.htm.

4. Chaves's research is published by Duke University in the National Congregations Study, https://sites.duke.edu/ncsweb. The data summarized here is from Kevin D. Dougherty, Mark Chaves, and Michael O. Emerson, "Racial Diversity in U.S. Congregations, 1998–2019," *Journal for the Scientific Study of Religion* (December 2020), https://sites.duke.edu/ncsweb/files/2020/10/Racial-Diversity-in-U.S.-Congregations-1998-2019.pdf.

5. "Pastors' Views on Racial Reconciliation: A Survey of American Protestant Pastors," Lifeway Research, September 2021, https://research.lifeway.com/wp-content/uploads/2022/02/Pastors -Sept-2021-Racial-Reconciliation-Report.pdf.

6. The Gospel Coalition, "A House Divided Cannot Stand," YouTube, April 20, 2018, 22:00, https://www.youtube.com/watch?v=-wmj0i1oH1Q.

7. Ibid.

8. The Gospel Coalition, "Don't Lose Heart: Why It's Worth It to Fight for Racial Harmony Even When We Don't See Progress," YouTube, April 17, 2018, https://www.youtube.com/watch?v=g9Mv5NJkjJE. Emphasis added.

CHAPTER 10: WHERE DO
MULTIETHNIC FAMILIES FIT IN?

1. By referring to "marriage" here and elsewhere, we are assuming Jesus's definition of one man and one woman becoming one flesh for one lifetime based on Matthew 19:4-6.

2. Sheryll Cashin, *Loving: Interracial Intimacy in America and the Threat to White Supremacy* (Boston: Beacon Press, 2017), 6.

3. "African American Adoptions," The Adoption History Project, University of Oregon Department of History, last updated February 24, 2012, https://pages.uoregon.edu/adoption/topics/AfricanAmerican.htm.

4. Margaret Carroll, "Should White Parents Be Allowed to Adopt Black Children? The Question Still Sparks Debate," *Chicago Tribune*, June 10, 1987, https://www.chicagotribune.com/news/ct-xpm-1987-06-10-8702130663-story.html.

5. Jason Lemon, "Why Ibram Kendi Is Facing a Backlash over a Tweet about Amy Coney Barrett's Adopted Haitian Children," *Newsweek*, September 27, 2020, https://www.newsweek.com/why-ibram-kendi-facing-backlash-over-tweet-about-amy-coney-barretts-adopted-haitian-children-1534507.

6. Alec Schemmel, "Former School Official Says She Would Abort Child before Letting White Evangelicals Adopt," Fox Illinois, May 24, 2022, https://foxillinois.com/news/nation-world/board-member-resigns-after-saying-shed-rather-see-baby-aborted-than-adopted-by-christians-san-diego-california-jo-luehmann.

7. Audrey Murph-Brown and Kim Stevens, "Being Anti-Racist: A Critical Way to Support Children of Color in Foster Care and Adoption," North American Council on Adoptable Children, September 17, 2020, https://nacac.org/resource/being-anti-racist-a-critical-way-to-support-children-of-color-in-foster-care-and-adoption.

8. Ibid.

9. Some LGBT advocates use similar reasoning in their call for adoption and foster placements into LGBT "families." But this is a category error. Race is a social construct, not a sin. People of different ethnicities or cultures coming together to form a family isn't a sin. Nor is it a sin for people of different ethnicities or cultures to raise a child of a different ethnicity or culture. In contrast, people of the same sex coming together to form a familial bond is a sin. It is against God's design for sex, marriage, and family.

10. David Figlio, "The Importance of a Diverse Teaching Force," Brookings Institute, November 16, 2017, https://www.brookings.edu/research/the-importance-of-a-diverse-teaching-force.

11. https://www.psychologytoday.com/us/blog/psychology-the-people/202112/why-representation-matters-and-why-it-s-still-not-enough.

CHAPTER 11: HOW DO WE TALK ABOUT RACE?

1. Layla F. Saad, *Me and White Supremacy: Combat Racism, Change the World, and Become a Good Ancestor* (Chicago: Sourcebooks, 2020), and Jemar Tisby, *How to Fight Racism: Courageous Christianity and the Journey Toward Racial Justice* (Grand Rapids: Zondervan, 2021).

2. Erik Ortiz, "Amber Guyger Found Guilty of Murder at Trial in Fatal Shooting of Neighbor Botham Jean," NBC News, October 1, 2019, https:// www.nbcnews.com/news/us-news/ amber-guyger-found-guilty-murder-trial-fatal-shooting-neighbor-botham-n1060506.

3. Jemar Tisby, "White Christians, Do Not Cheapen the Hug and Message of Forgiveness from Botham Jean's Brother," *Washington Post*, October 3, 2019, https://www.washingtonpost.com/religion /2019/10/03/white-christians-do-not-cheapen-hug-message-forgiveness-botham-jeans-brother.

ACKNOWLEDGMENTS

Writing a book is definitely a group project. Many skills were needed to get us across the finish line.

First and foremost, we want to thank the Lord for entrusting this ministry to us. We are humbled by all we have been able to do so far, and we are committed to riding this wave together as long as the Lord agrees.

Jane Pantig and Thaddeus Williams, thank you for your encouragement and wisdom as we've launched the Center for Biblical Unity. We have made a good team.

We would like to thank our sister Julie Smyth for her consistent encouragement to write this book over the last two years. Her experience in Christian publishing was invaluable as she cheered us on during the writing process. She helped us believe in ourselves, even when we felt like we were underqualified for the task. She also acted as the developmental editor for the book before its submission to the publisher. She is largely responsible for bringing cohesion to the manuscript, despite it having two authors with two very different writing styles.

To our Harvest House family: Thank you! Thank you for seeing the benefit and beauty of our project. Thank you for coming alongside and walking with us to bring *Walking in Unity* to fruition. We are blessed to be in this with you all.

Natasha Crain (a.k.a.: Tasha gurrl!), thank you for your prayers, advice, and for connecting us with Harvest House. We are grateful for your friendship.

We both greatly benefited from "the aunty," Alisa Childers, as she walked with us on this journey. She even let Monique live in her basement and cooked her meals for three weeks so she could focus on completing the first draft of the manuscript. Alisa's interview with Monique in June 2018 not only helped to launch our ministry, but her friendship and prayers have sustained us during discouraging seasons.

Thank you to our brothers Jeremy Bannister, Brett Kunkle, and Jason Smith for spiritually shepherding us. We appreciate your godly love and guidance.

Thank you to all our Center for Biblical Unity family who gave on Giving Tuesday 2022 to make this book possible. We would not be here without your generosity!

Monique would also like to thank Uncle Virgil Walker, Uncle Voddie Baucham, Cousin Dr. Neil Shenvi, and Uncle Dr. Pat Sawyer, who all played important roles in her journey toward a more excellent understanding of the Scriptures.

Grace and peace,
Monique and Krista

ABOUT THE AUTHORS

Krista Bontrager is an author, a podcaster, and the vice president of Educational Programs and Biblical Integrity at the Center for Biblical Unity. With a BA in communications from Biola University and MAs in theology and Bible exposition from the Talbot School of Theology, Krista has worked in the fields of theology and apologetics for almost three decades. She is pursuing a DMin in apologetics at Birmingham Theological Seminary.

Monique Duson is the president at the Center for Biblical Unity. Formerly an advocate of critical race theory (CRT), Monique now actively speaks out against the use of CRT within the church. She has appeared on shows such as *Relatable with Allie Beth Stuckey*, the *Alisa Childers Podcast*, and *Breakpoint with John Stonestreet*. Monique is working toward a MA in public theology at Birmingham Theological Seminary.

To learn more about Harvest House books and
to read sample chapters, visit our website:

www.HarvestHousePublishers.com

HARVEST HOUSE PUBLISHERS
EUGENE, OREGON